21 97 003A

COMFORT FOR DEPRESSION

Catalogued - For CHAUHAN-FAMILY LIBRARY
02NOV- 2003

D0958763

Overcoming Common Problems Series

The ABC of Eating
Coping with anorexia, bulimia and
compulsive eating
JOY MELVILLE

An A–Z of Alternative Medicine
BRENT Q. HAFEN AND KATHRYN J.
FRANDSEN

Arthritis
Is your suffering really necessary?
DR WILLIAM FOX

Being the Boss
STEPHEN FITZSIMON

Birth Over Thirty
SHEILA KITZINGER

Body Language
How to read others' thoughts by their gestures
ALLAN PEASE

Calm Down
How to cope with frustration and anger
DR PAUL HAUCK

Comfort for Depression
JANET HORWOOD

Common Childhood Illnesses
DR PATRICIA GILBERT

Complete Public Speaker
GILES BRANDRETH

Coping with Depression and Elation
DR PATRICK McKEON

Coping Successfully with Your Child's Asthma
DR PAUL CARSON

**Coping Successfully with Your Child's Skin
Problems**
DR PAUL CARSON

**Coping Successfully with Your Hyperactive
Child**
DR PAUL CARSON

Curing Arthritis Cookbook
MARGARET HILLS

Curing Arthritis – The Drug-free Way
MARGARET HILLS

Curing Illness – The Drug-free Way
MARGARET HILLS

Depression
DR PAUL HAUCK

Divorce and Separation
ANGELA WILLANS

The Epilepsy Handbook
SHELAGH McGOVERN

Everything You Need to Know about Adoption
MAGGIE JONES

**Everything You Need to Know about Contact
Lenses**
DR ROBERT YOUNGSON

**Everything You Need to Know about the
Pill**
WENDY COOPER AND TOM SMITH

Everything You Need to Know about Shingles
DR ROBERT YOUNGSON

Family First Aid and Emergency Handbook
DR ANDREW STANWAY

Feverfew
A traditional herbal remedy for migraine and
arthritis
DR STEWART JOHNSON

Fight Your Phobia and Win
DAVID LEWIS

Flying Without Fear
TESSA DUCKWORTH AND DAVID
MILLER

Goodbye Backache
DR DAVID IMRIE WITH COLLEEN
DIMSON

Good Publicity Guide
REGINALD PEPLOW

Helping Children Cope with Grief
ROSEMARY WELLS

How to Be Your Own Best Friend
DR PAUL HAUCK

How to Control your Drinking
DRS W. MILLER AND R. MUNOZ

Overcoming Common Problems Series

Overcoming Common Problems Series

Overcoming Common Problems

COMFORT FOR DEPRESSION

Janet Horwood

SHELDON PRESS
LONDON

First published in Great Britain in 1982 by
George Allen and Unwin, under the title *Comfort*

Copyright © Janet Horwood 1982 & 1988

This edition published in 1988 by Sheldon Press,
SPCK, Marylebone Road, London NW1 4DU

Second impression 1988

All rights reserved. No part of this book may be
reproduced or transmitted in any form or by any
means, electronic or mechanical, including photocopying,
recording, or by any information storage and retrieval
system, without permission in writing from the publisher.

British Library Cataloguing in Publication Data

Horwood, Janet
  Comfort for depression.—2nd ed.—
  (Overcoming common problems).
  1. Depression, Mental—Treatment
  2. Self-care, Health
  I. Title   II. Series
  616.85'2706   RC537

ISBN 0–85969–554–9

Photoset by Deltatype, Ellesmere Port
and printed in Great Britain by
Richard Clay Ltd, Bungay, Suffolk

To John, Joseph, Rachel and Jonathan

Contents

Foreword

Most of the people who write to me at *Woman* are depressed in one way or another. Maybe their marriages aren't working; maybe they're lonely – and it's because they're depressed they've got trapped in a vicious circle. No one wants to know them because they're gloomy; they're gloomy because no one wants to know them. They may be depressed because they're not relaxed and tension and stress is exhausting them; maybe they're depressed because they have money worries, relationship worries or problems at work. Certainly some of the people who write to me *do* need to see a doctor to be prescribed proper medication to help them; others might be helped by seeing a counsellor or even a psychiatrist to sort out their problems. But the vast majority are just feeling miserable like you and I and everyone in the world feels gloomy and depressed from time to time. So what's the way to help them?

Most of the books on depression and stress are written by doctors – invariably with a medical axe to grind, which is fine if you're suffering from clinical depression. But often you need something less specialized. And something, too, that doesn't send you running with panic to the surgery for something to 'help with your hormones' or something to 'suppress your amine inhibitors'. What you need is an everyday book for everyday people and one, too, that doesn't leave you high and dry with those bleak instructions to 'pamper yourself', 'be good to yourself', 'love yourself' – all incredibly difficult to put into practice if you're feeling low. There's no more depressing farewell from a friend who smiles, gives you a wave and tells you to 'take care of yourself'. It's just not that easy. Or maybe some well-meaning person might suggest, 'take a holiday'. But maybe you haven't the money, there's no one to look after the kids, it's not a suitable time to go away, or you just don't fancy going away by yourself. And anyway, the problems will still be there when you get home. What you need is a way of giving yourself a holiday while still staying at home – a holiday from your anxious, unhappy self.

Here at last is the answer. Janet Horwood gives you kind, sensible

1

and practical advice on exactly how to go about cheering yourself up when you feel down.

There's a special need for a book like this these days. Anxieties hound us – from unemployment to wider world problems like nuclear war. As Paul Valery said, 'The trouble with our times is that the future is not what it used to be.' True, more material comforts may be available – but only to some. And just *not* having those things we see every day on the television – a job, yearly holidays, a car, a television, even fitted carpets – can make us feel unhappy and deprived. And because of our current obsession to have our own things, our own rooms, our own privacy, our 'own space', as they are always advocating in the States, when we're down and miserable often there's no one there to see how unhappy we are. And no one around to give us the comfort we want.

Even if you're in a family, life can seem comfortless, particularly if you're a woman. I so often get letters from women who say they spend all their time looking after their families – but there seems to be no one to look after *them* when they feel low and sad.

When we feel down we become like small children. Like small children we need good, constructive, comforting advice from a parent. But it's one thing to wail, 'I want my mum!' when we're children; quite another when we're adults. Failing mum – read this book. It's as happy and helpful as a good old-fashioned cuddle!

Virginia Ironside
Problem Page Editor, Woman

1

Why Do You Need Comfort?

We all experience perfect days. Days when, whatever the weather or the circumstances, we feel glad to be alive and can cope with anything that comes along.

But there are also days when the world truly seems out of joint. Though the sun blazes down from a cloudless sky, it could be raining for all we care. Everyone else seems rushed, bad-tempered, self-absorbed. Even if we are surrounded by other people, we feel alone, isolated. Food tastes like sawdust and even the smallest task seems too much effort. In short, we are depressed.

If you have picked up this book, the chances are that's how you feel now. What you are desperately searching for is some kind of comfort.

Comfort is that wonderful soothing feeling you get when someone you love dearly holds you close. It can also come from the total relaxation of sinking into a hot bath, or from eating a certain kind of food or listening to a special piece of music.

Whatever the source of comfort it can temporarily make you forget your pain and misery as you lose yourself in gentle oblivion.

The mistake many people make is to assume that masses of comfort will solve a problem; that soothing the pain will make it go away altogether. It won't do that, of course – the problem still has to be worked out. What comfort *can* do is to give you those much needed breathers, a chance to gather your strength together and face reality.

Used wisely, comfort will help you – especially if you can understand what is going on and why you feel so down, and know how you are going to cope with it.

One of the strongest emotions linked with depression is fear. Fear of facing the causes makes you want to ignore your misery, cover it up and hope it will go away. But just as you cannot overlook a raging temperature, so it is impossible to turn your back on depression.

Equally, fear makes you cling to your depression – fear of change, of looking ahead and seeing what the future might be like. There is plenty of comfort – of the wrong sort – to be found in thinking like this.

So one of the things you are going to have to do is face up to your fear and your depression. Think of it as something positive. It is often only when they feel really down that people have the opportunity to examine themselves and their lives. Your depression is going to help you to know yourself better, find out who you are, who you would like to be – who you can be, if you want to.

You have a tough time ahead and that's where the comfort will come into its own. It will allow you to work through your problems less painfully; in some cases it will simply soothe you, in others it will actively encourage you to progress.

The Reality of Depression

People get depressed for all sorts of reasons. Although the pain is sharper after a major tragedy, the duller, prolonged pain of a less obvious depression can be just as damaging – in both cases you have a duty to yourself to live through the pain and learn from it.

When you know exactly why you are down you are already halfway to recovery. Because the cause is obvious you can devote all your energy towards working through your depression.

It is also easier to recognise that you will go through various emotional stages before you come out the other side. Knowing what these are is important.

Ten to one, your depression has been triggered off by a major crisis in your life. Someone you love may have died, your marriage or an affair may have broken up, maybe you've been sacked from your job or made redundant or have got severe money problems.

Even having some warning of these things makes little difference. You may have talked about leaving home and getting a divorce for months or years, but when it happens it still comes as a terrible shock.

So your first reaction is one of numbness. You can't believe that it has happened; you don't want to believe it. You go around in a daze, automatically doing your usual tasks without even thinking about what you are doing. You have no feelings left.

4

Then the numbness gives way to anger, bitterness and real misery – you find yourself crying out 'Why should this happen to me? It's not fair, I don't deserve this!' Many people suppress their feelings at this stage – though they are thinking bitter, vindictive thoughts they don't express them because they are ashamed of their violence. In fact, these feelings are perfectly normal and it is important not to crush them.

The next stage is overwhelming sadness. You feel desperately sorry for yourself. You lose respect for what you are, and it really doesn't seem worth bothering to make life more bearable.

Gradually you go further and further downhill into an all-pervading lethargy where everything is just too much for you to cope with.

Added to all this, you find that most of your friends are beginning to lose patience and telling you to pull yourself together, look on the bright side, count your blessings, and other meaningless clichés that don't help at all.

So now you need to lean heavily on all sorts of comfort, to give you that extra strength to pull through to the final stage of acceptance. Acceptance doesn't mean sitting back and giving in. It means coming to terms with what has happened, seeing both the positive and negative sides, and realising that you have learnt through suffering.

If you are not sure why you are depressed in some ways you have a harder task. The causes may be so deep inside you or so far away in the past that it is going to take some hard work to dig them out.

All you know at the moment is that you feel generally dissatisfied with yourself and your life. When you wake in the morning you feel tired, but by the end of the day you are unable to sleep. Even if you do sleep like a log, you wake up feeling you could do with a few more hours in bed. Perhaps you get a lot of minor illnesses – colds, headaches, flu, backache.

You need comfort too. Though you can't pinpoint a major crisis to justify your depression, there are nevertheless areas of your life that are out of key.

Once you've checked with your doctor that there is nothing radically wrong with your health, set aside half an hour or so alone.

Sit down and make a list of everything that is dissatisfying in your life – anything that might be contributing to your mood.

For instance, is your relationship with your partner going through a tricky patch – do you feel trapped or uneasy about it? Is your social life uninspired, or your job boring, or are you feeling put upon at home with too many demands being made and no time for yourself?

Writing things down will give you a starting point, and may reveal something that's depressed you in the past but that you pushed out of sight at the time.

Once you have pinned down the problem you can start to use comfort to work your way through it, in the same way as someone facing a major tragedy.

How Comfort Can Help You

All sorts of comfort are suggested in this book and obviously not all of the ideas will be right for you. But beware of stereotyping yourself. You may *think* that you can only find comfort alone, but it is still worth giving the social aspects a try, especially if being alone hasn't always worked well in the past.

Above all, now is the time in your life when you must put yourself first occasionally. For a while you are going to concentrate on *your* needs and desires. It won't be easy, especially if you haven't done it for years. People will complain. But if you are gently firm about what you want they will come to respect your strength of purpose.

Don't ever allow yourself to feel guilty about indulging yourself while you are working through your depression. Remember that the result will be a happier you, and that can only make those around you happier as well. Obviously you are not going to withdraw from life altogether, but if you want the ideas in this book to work you must be absolutely firm with yourself and others. You need the comfort, you need it now, and nothing must stand in your way.

2
Getting Through the Day

It's morning. You've spent a sleepless night tossing and turning, dropping occasionally into a fitful doze. You finally dropped into a deep slumber just before the alarm went or the children rushed in. Now you have got to get up and face yet another day.

You dread the thought. Not only are you feeling down, you are tired as well. How can you possibly drag yourself through the day?

Starting the Day Right

However black things may be, try and begin each day as well as possible – in a way that is right for you and will give you the best start. If you feel like crying – do so for a while, and then make yourself get up. Even if you have always been the type to leap out of bed, try getting up slowly. Have a good stretch first. Let your body, as well as your mind, adapt to the idea of getting up.

It's a good idea to have a radio or tape recorder in the bedroom; as soon as you wake up, put on your favourite, cheerful tape or find a music station on the radio. Avoid the news programmes – you can do without knowing the state of the world for a while.

Don't spend the vital first few moments of the day in unrelieved gloom. As soon as you get up, open the curtains. Unless the weather is really appalling, fling open the window and take six deep breaths.

Now you are ready to go on to the next stage. Even if you had a bath the night before, have another one now – or, even better, have a shower if you can.

If you usually go around in a dressing gown until after breakfast try getting dressed and ready before breakfast.

Your methods of coping with early morning will depend to some extent on whether you are alone or not.

If you are alone you can indulge yourself. When you have that bath you can lie and soak for a while. When people are depressed they are often tense as well, so aim to create a relaxed atmosphere, even if it means getting up ten minutes earlier.

When you dress, choose your favourite clothes, the ones you feel most comfortable in. If it is cold put on an extra layer so that you feel really warm all day.

If you are alone for the first time in years, it hurts. Everything you do reminds you of what your life used to be like. You may feel comforted by keeping the old routines, but if they hurt, do try to vary things. If you always used to have breakfast first, try getting dressed and showered beforehand. If you always listened to the news over breakfast, listen to music instead.

If you are not alone, and have a partner, parents or children making various demands, starting the day peacefully can be more difficult. The trouble is that when you are down you are not very good company – you are bound to be snappish or morose. Your mood will affect them, and then you'll feel guilty.

There are ways round this. Try getting up half an hour before everyone else. That way you'll have a little peace and quiet just for you – time to get your thoughts together, to meditate, do exercises, have a quiet bath, read, even cry. It may seem crazy to deprive yourself of sleep, but on the plus side you'll feel less tense, less put upon, less resentful.

Mornings can be bad times even in the happiest of families. Everyone is in a rush and time races, making dressing a chore, breakfast a hassle.

What you are aiming to do is get rid of all the small things that create unhappiness and tension – you have enough to cope with as it is. One time saver is to put all clothes out ready the night before and lay the breakfast table; that way there'll be less to do in the morning.

On the days when your mood is blackest make a few simple requests. If you aren't usually brought a cup of tea or glass of orange juice in bed, now is the time to ask.

If your partner is around to help with the children, ask him or her to take over completely occasionally. Make it clear that while they are sorting themselves out you are not available – as if you weren't in the house at all. Don't push your luck on this one, though; one morning a week done with good grace is better than every morning done resentfully.

The Rest of the Day

With breakfast over, the day is well on the way. One of the major side effects when you are in the dumps is the overwhelming feeling that nothing is worth bothering about. It is easy to forget that, whatever has happened, it is you and you alone who control your life and that you can make each day worth living, although the pain of achieving this is often hard to bear.

How you spend each day will depend on whether you are at home or at work.

If you are at home. Your home should work for you, whether it is a two-room flat or a 22-room mansion. When you are depressed you need somewhere where you can relax and feel comforted with all your possessions around you. The trouble is, you've probably let things slide – papers all over the place, clothes in the wrong drawers, washing-up in the sink. You look round you and despair. You wander aimlessly from room to room or sit slumped in one chair with neither the energy nor the inclination to do anything about it.

In this case, your home is working against you. It's a trite expression, but there really should be a place for everything. If your home is well organised, without being fanatically tidy, it will be a place you can relax in. As far as you yourself are concerned, what you want to gain out of each day is a feeling of progress, of having achieved something, however small.

Make a list of what needs doing and aim to tackle one item each day. What you want initially is one room in the house where you can go and fling yourself down without having to worry about doing anything to it. Decide which is your favourite room in the house, the one you feel most at ease in, and make it your priority. You can get your various possessions into some sort of order by buying brightly-coloured files for all your papers, going through your books and sorting them into alphabetical or subject order, going through your clothes and throwing out the ones you know you'll never want to wear again, and getting hold of some small boxes for storing things like jewellery and make-up.

You may be the sort of person who gets a lot of pleasure from cleaning – it works for some. The physical effort of polishing brass or silver, scrubbing the oven or kitchen floor, cleaning all the windows, can be very absorbing and also helps get rid of aggression.

During the day give yourself several short breaks when you do something different – ten minutes with your feet up reading the paper, doing the crossword or just lying quietly listening to music. Don't skip lunch, and don't just eat a quick snack standing up in the kitchen. Depression makes people lose respect for themselves but you are worth a place set at the table and a proper meal, even if it's only a light one.

When you've got at least one room in order you can start improving on it. Try moving the furniture into a different position. Add some bright touches. Even if there isn't much money to spare you can afford to splash out on a bunch of flowers or a pot plant, a new print for the wall, some brightly coloured candles for the evenings, some material to cover a cushion. More ambitiously, think about some redecorating – but don't overreach yourself. If you've never wallpapered before, papering a large room is a daunting prospect. But a few tins of emulsion paint can do wonders for a drab room and take very little time to apply. If you only use some rooms in the evenings adapt them accordingly. Perhaps the lighting doesn't seem quite right for instance. You can avoid harsh lighting by using table lamps or spotlights, softening lampshades or pink bulbs. You could have dimmer switches, too, so that you can vary the intensity of the lighting.

If you've got a garden get out there, even in winter. Lose yourself in weeding, planting, mowing the lawn. Spring is the time of year when a lot of people feel low, and planting seeds and small plants is a good way to give you hope for the future.

If you haven't got a garden, you can grow plants in window boxes. Have one outside your bedroom window and change the plants according to the time of year. That way, even if your window looks out on to drab buildings you'll have greenery to relieve the gloom.

When you are at home all day there is a temptation to sit around feeling lethargic, but if you can make yourself achieve one thing each day, it will lift your spirits. At the end of the day you'll be able to look back and say, 'Well, I did get my papers in order/sort out the clothes/plant some spinach seeds' and you'll feel your time has not been wasted. If you give in to doing nothing, if you let your home become a burden, then you will not only feel depressed, you'll feel guilty too – and you've got enough on your plate without that emotion as well.

If you have to go out to work. Going out to work can cover up your misery, on the surface at least. But there will still be many times during the day when you find it hard to concentrate and feel your brain is being scattered in all directions.

Of course, it could be that you are unhappy because you don't enjoy what you are doing, in which case now is the time to start thinking seriously about making a break (see chapter 3). But whatever your feelings about your job, you are committed to spending several hours a day doing it, and you want to make this time as enjoyable as possible.

Start by improving your journey to work. If you drive and have to cope with rush hour traffic, try leaving a little earlier to avoid it. In any case, it's often a good idea to get into work before other people – in the same way as that half an hour to yourself at home relieves tension, so does half an hour getting yourself sorted out for the working day ahead. If you haven't got a radio or cassette in the car it's well worth getting one – you are less likely to get wound up over the traffic if your mind is on a radio talk or some music.

If you travel to work on the bus or train, always take something to read. If you haven't already done so, try and make your work area more relaxing and personal. Take in pictures from home, buy a few picture postcards or posters to put up on the wall, and a bunch of flowers to put on the desk each week.

At lunchtime try and get out. Arrange lunch with friends, visit the local museum or art gallery, take a walk in the local park. But make it a walk with a purpose, not an aimless ramble. Make a point of identifying the trees, flowers or birds you see. Or walk round your town or city, visiting places you've never bothered about before. If your job is hectic or noisy spend the lunch hour sitting quietly in a church or find out whether there are any lunchtime concerts or plays

11

to go to. If you are tempted to wander round the shops, do so again with a purpose. Perhaps buy something small for yourself, such as a new belt, a scarf, a tie, or a book, or something for the home – some brightly coloured or scented candles for the evenings, or some joss sticks. If you haven't planned an evening meal you can buy for that. Even if there's still some stew left over, aim to cheer up the meal by buying an exotic fruit or vegetable.

Don't drink too much at lunchtime. It's tempting to drown your sorrows. But you'll just feel sleepy during the afternoon and the hangover will hit you when you get home.

A Day in Bed

There is another alternative to facing the day when you wake up, and that is not to get up at all, to spend the whole day in bed. But if you do this you must do it positively. After all, most of us only spend the day in bed when we're ill, never when we are physically fit. So it's a special occasion.

Ideally, you should plan ahead for this day so that you get the most out of it. It shouldn't be something that just happens because you've had a bad night. We all get tired and when we are depressed we feel even more exhausted. Your day in bed is going to help give you back some of that physical strength you need.

The night before, tidy your bedroom. Put away all clothes, and bits and pieces that clutter up the room. Put fresh sheets on the bed and wear clean nightclothes. Sort out what you are likely to need the next day – books, radio, tape recorder, and so on.

When you wake up in the morning you will have a moment of dread, but then you can relax. Today is the day when you are not going to get up! At this point you will probably doze off gratefully and when you next wake the morning will be half gone. If you can, now is the time to get up – but only briefly. Regard yourself as a sort of convalescent. Have a long, slow, deep bath. Do your hair, shave or whatever, put on perfume or aftershave, make the bed, then get back in. Bliss. Now you can read, listen to the radio, eat if you feel like it. Treat yourself to a light lunch and remove the tray afterwards. Draw the curtains, take the phone off the hook and sleep for a while. If you can organise your sleeping time it's better than dozing on and off – but if that suits you better then do it. This is *your* day, so enjoy it. Make sure you have plenty of pillows to prop yourself up and if it's cold make a hot water bottle. Try and keep the room warm – you can economise by switching off heating in all the other rooms.

When evening comes draw the curtains. Have another bath or shower. Create a warm atmosphere in the bedroom by lighting candles and burning joss sticks.

The only major drawback to a day spent like this is that you may not be able to sleep at night. Well, you are going to have to be philosophical about that. Your body is well rested after a day in bed. Sleep would be ideal but if this is impossible (and see chapter 10 for some solutions) then don't panic – a night without much sleep after a day of total rest is not a disaster.

Whether you've stayed in bed or got up as usual, you have made it through the day. If you've used some of the ideas in this chapter, you'll have coped practically with the process. The next four chapters suggest ways of enhancing and building on this practical basis and giving yourself the comfort you need so badly at the moment.

3

Indulge Your Mind

Depression is a very powerful emotion. It can take you over completely, and very quickly. It seeps into every part of your mind and stays there, if you let it. Though other thoughts force themselves through that grey blanket of gloom at odd moments, they vanish all too quickly. And there you are right down in the depths again.

With depression, as with so many other things, you need to keep a sense of balance. On the one hand you are not going to suppress or even fight off your painful feelings, but on the other you will benefit far more if you remain in control of what is going on.

It is definitely a challenge. Part of your mind won't want to be made to feel better. It wants to carry on feeling the pain. But another part of you craves comfort and relief. Realise now that feeling depressed is a very passive state of mind. You probably notice its effect in physical ways. You move slowly, feel tired, react erratically and even have minor accidents like dropping cups or plates, breaking things, or burning food, to reinforce the knowledge that your mind is only half on the basic process of day-to-day living. You also find it hard to concentrate or make decisions, even simple ones like what to eat in the evening, where to go over the weekend, whether to accept an invitation or not.

However bad you are feeling right now, never forget how important your mind is. When it is healthy and happy it can bring you so much joy, pleasure and fulfilment. You owe it to your mind to care for it now, so that eventually it will be healed.

You can take up the challenge to care for your mind in all sorts of ways but the main one here is that you are going to indulge it. You are going to let it have its feelings of sadness and at the same time use those feelings to create a mood that will gradually become more optimistic.

How You Feel Now

Are you at your lowest ebb so far? Your grief, misery, despair at their strongest? At times the pain may actually make you feel totally numbed. At other times your unhappiness is so acute and agonising that you long for some sort of oblivion, some way in which you can switch off your mind.

When you have these feelings it is hard to remember what life was like before disaster struck. It seems as if you have always felt like this – and certainly the possibility that you will ever again be relaxed and happy seems remote.

Your days and nights are dominated mostly by thoughts of what triggered off this pain. If you dare, metaphorically, to raise your head to look into the future, the prospect is so bleak and never-endingly depressing that you stop bothering.

What You Can Do About It

First of all, a few thoughts.

Don't forget, that you have every right to feel pain. It is all part of being human. But you also have a right to feel happy.

Unfortunately this particular right won't come of its own accord – you have to make it happen and remember that you are in sole control of your happiness or misery. Outside circumstances may intrude but cannot always be blamed – at least, not in the long term. The danger lies in clinging on to miserable feelings and getting so used to having them around that life without them starts to seem insecure and frightening.

If you let this happen you are not allowing yourself to run your own life. You are allowing outside circumstances like a bereavement, divorce, or a boring job to rule you and make you unhappy, while all the time, within you, you have the ability to be happy.

You are much more likely to achieve happiness if you realise that the pain you are suffering now is not a totally negative emotion and that through it you will learn more about yourself and those around you; that through it your mind can grow and develop.

What You Can Do Practically

Have you let yourself go yet? Or have you decided that on the surface you are going to be very brave. Suppressing your feelings in this way is a bad trap to fall into, though most of us are brought up to do just that.

Think back to your childhood, watch your own children or any other young child and notice how very close to the surface their emotions are. If something goes wrong they immediately cry or stamp their feet in rage or unhappiness. A few moments later it's all over.

But usually only very young children give vent to their emotions in this way. Once they go to school they stop showing their feelings so dramatically, and by the time adulthood is reached the obvious emotions have been neatly suppressed. For the rest of their lives they spend their time concealing their true feelings. When people upset them unnecessarily, they grin and bear it; if there's trouble from the boss at work, they bend over backwards to keep the peace.

But if you are suffering pain you have every right to express it – by having a really good cry, for instance.

If you have felt yourself on the verge of tears for days but have so far failed to cry properly, then you must stop holding back, even if you haven't cried since you were a child.

How To Cry

It isn't easy if you are not used to crying, and you will probably find it much better to cry alone if you feel at all embarrassed. So the first rule is to make sure you are not going to be disturbed for a while.

Concentrate on all the saddest aspects of your life. If it helps you can write them down or speak them aloud or into a tape recorder. Or find some romantic poetry to read or listen to music that has always moved you in the past. Immerse yourself in the feelings these evoke.

You may find a lump coming into your throat and habit will make you swallow hard to stop the feeling going any further. This time don't stop yourself, don't switch off, let yourself go right to the end of this particular emotional road, relax and let the tears fall.

If you can cry fairly easily you may prefer to have a close friend with you some of the time. Being held tightly while you cry is obviously very comforting – but the tears themselves provide comfort too. As you cry let your body go, lie on the floor or bed, hug a pillow or cushion close to you, and think of the release that those tears are providing. They seem to be washing your mind clear and if you haven't cried for a long time you may be surprised at how much better you feel afterwards.

A lot of people don't let themselves cry because they are afraid that once they start they won't be able to stop. If you do find you can't stop crying for a long time, don't worry about it – it is what your mind needs at the moment.

But maybe you have done all the crying and now your main emotions are of anger or bitterness. These need to be expressed too but again you may be afraid of unleashing all your violent feelings.

But expressing your anger is just as important as expressing your sadness. You may be angry with someone who has hurt you or with yourself for allowing it to happen, or just with the world in general.

Of course life is not fair. It deals us blows all the time. Other people seem to get away with murder while we are left to suffer and cope with our anger.

You can think your anger out of your mind by being rational and realising that no one has any right to let you feel like this, least of all yourself. But you may also need, especially in the early stages, to openly express your anger.

When was the last time you screamed, really screamed? Most of us get pushed to what we call screaming pitch, but we don't allow ourselves actually to cry out because it is not socially acceptable.

If you can organise a good scream, so much the better. Of course, you need to find a deserted spot or scream into a pillow, otherwise all the good it does you will be outbalanced by the neighbours complaining or your family worrying.

At first you will find it hard. Your throat will tense up and a small squeak will come out. But if you persevere to a full-throated scream it will release a lot of pent-up tensions.

Your feelings of anger may also make you feel physically violent, as if you could quite easily lash out at the next person you meet. Before this happens, recognise your violent longings and organise them. Hit a pillow, a cushion, the mattress, pummelling into them with your fists. Smash an old piece of crockery.

As well as wordless screaming, you may find it helpful to sound off verbally. Perhaps you can sound off at a partner or a good friend who loves and cares about you, who understands how you feel, and who will not try to stop you but will let you do all the talking and explaining.

If you let yourself go emotionally in these ways the danger is that afterwards you may feel ashamed. You have behaved 'childishly'. But it is not childish to say what you feel or even to show your pain. We were all children once and our adult selves are a combination of all the feelings and experiences we have had since birth. You need never feel ashamed of acknowledging the continuing existence of the child in you, and taking from it whatever it has to offer. What you have done is to take the sort of behaviour more commonly found in children and refined it as an adult, because as you cried, screamed or threw dishes, you knew exactly why you were behaving in this way and how such behaviour could help.

Other Suggestions

As well as allowing your mind to comfort itself by expressing its pain, you also need to provide it with the cosseting it needs. This can come from allowing it a breathing space, a chance to switch off for a while.

The sort of comfort you choose will depend on the reasons for your depression, and on analysing them if they are not immediately apparent.

If you have made one room in your house especially comfortable, this could come into its own if you feel depressed but can't understand why. Maybe you lead what on the surface seems to be an ideal life – plenty going on around you with a busy job or family commitments, each day filled to the corners with things to do. But is it that ideal? Many people who live like this get depressed for the very simple reason that at no time do they have a breathing space. Constant demands are being made on them; the days, weeks, months and even years go past and there never seems to be a moment when they can be alone for a while to get their thoughts together.

Maybe this has happened to you almost without you realising it. If so, a quarter of an hour each day in your comfortable room could help tremendously. You are going to have to be very firm with those who share your home and life – once you go into that room on no account are you to be disturbed.

18

A room like this can also be a place for retreat if you are depressed for other reasons – you can use it for peace, for finding out about yourself, for working slowly through your sadness.

Once you are alone in your room you have to decide how to spend the time. What you are after is a way of diverting your thoughts for a while, of allowing your mind, which has probably been under terrific strain, to get a rest without actually going to sleep.

The answer could lie in meditation. All sorts of claims are made for meditation – that it improves your health, lowers blood pressure, slows the heart beat and, most important of all, that it soothes the mind.

If you have never tried to meditate before don't be put off by any mystery that surrounds it. Some people like to make meditation sound mystical and it is true that experienced meditators can reach levels far beyond those experienced by the average person. But all you are aiming for is a few minutes during which your mind will be cleared of all thoughts and worries.

How To Meditate

Prepare yourself by taking the phone off the hook and barring everyone from entering the room. Make the atmosphere round you more restful, by lighting a joss stick if you like the smell, and by making sure the lighting is dim. During the day you can draw the curtains. At night you can use candles for lighting.

Try to have your sessions either before a major meal or at least an hour afterwards. Ideal times are first thing in the morning, before breakfast, just before lunch or last thing at night. If you try to meditate immediately after a meal, especially a large one, you may find it harder to relax.

So now you are ready. You won't need more than ten minutes to start with. Have a clock in the room, provided the tick isn't too loud, or take off your wrist watch and put it where you can see it easily.

First of all, you need to be comfortable. Sit in a chair that supports your back well and allows you to place both feet flat on the floor. Or sit on the floor cross-legged with your hands on your knees, or lie flat on your back, arms by your sides, legs straight with feet falling outwards.

19

You can keep your eyes open or closed, depending on the form of meditation you are going to use. Breathe in and out, slowly and deeply, through your nose. Think about each breath – as you breathe out imagine yourself clearing out all the debris from your body and mind, all the stress and tension, all the bitter and unhappy thoughts. As you breathe in, visualise this breath as fresh, new and healthy, bringing only good feelings with it.

This is the basis of meditation, but because it so difficult for ordinary human beings to control their minds and clear them completely, you will need some sort of prop, a substitute if you like, something which will fill your mind and keep unhappy thoughts at bay.

People who practise transcendental meditation are given a 'mantra', a special word which they repeat over and over again to exclude all other thoughts. You can choose your own mantra – it can be a word, a phrase, a sentence, or even several sentences. Choose it carefully, and go for something that has a good sound or meaning. Or if you want a series of words you could use the Lord's Prayer, a verse from one of the psalms or a favourite poem.

If you prefer not to use words you can try humming on a continuous note – aaaah, ummmmmm – or simply counting your breaths, one for each breath in and out, then two and so on. It is best to count up to four and then start all over again.

Another possibility is to have a plant or flower in the room. Place it in front of you where you can see it clearly. When you start your meditation fix your eyes and mind on this flower. Look at each petal and stamen as if you've never seen anything like it before. Examine the leaves, the colour, the way the veins run, how it is joined to the stem. After a while allow your mind to wander slightly on to other aspects of flowers or plants – you may wish to think about fruit, bees or whatever – but keep within this subject.

You can do the same exercise by staring deep in to a candle flame, or the flames of an open fire if you have one.

Whatever method of support you choose for your meditation you will find it hard at first to concentrate wholly on it. Other thoughts will constantly nag at you. The best way to deal with them is to adopt a sort of don't care attitude. It's as if you were saying to those thoughts, 'I know you are there but I'm not interested'. With practice you will find they intrude less frequently.

At the end of your session – stretch and then stand up slowly and take three deep, controlled breaths before you leave the room.

If you have tried meditation and feel it is not for you then you can still use that time to comfort your mind, but in different ways. You don't have to be alone for some of these – do what you feel would be best.

For instance, when did you last have a really good laugh? Often when people are really down it seems almost sacrilege to laugh and maybe you don't want to in case no one will believe you are really miserable. But laughter and tears are both good strong emotions and just because laughter is usually associated with happiness doesn't mean you should be deprived of it now.

Make a point of switching on the radio or television to catch the better comedy programmes. Borrow or buy tapes or records. Head for books that have amused you in the past. Even if you only laugh once it will be worth it.

You can also soothe your mind by listening to music. Choose something bright and cheerful and if you have headphones use them to let the music go right into your head and become part of you. If you can read music get hold of the full score for a symphony and follow it.

Go on a reading binge. You don't have to buy books, you can borrow them from the library. If you haven't read anything with a good story and solid ending for years do so now – detective stories, romantic fiction, historical novels, biographies, classic fiction are all a good way of losing yourself for a while.

If you find you can't even concentrate on a book, try looking at a picture in the room or in a book. Choose something with people and plenty of action. If you live in the centre of a town or city and can see the main road from your window, spend ten minutes or so just staring at the people going by. Think about what they are doing, wearing, saying.

If you really find it impossible to get any sort of comfort for your mind at home then you must plan to go away and do so. You could organise a simple country walk for yourself, or book a weekend or a few days in some form of retreat. You can choose a retreat in which you discuss your problems with others, or a silent form of retreat where you only meet others at meal and official prayer times.

Allow Yourself To Look Ahead

Perhaps at this time you are having to face up to making decisions about the future. You have come to a crossroads in your life, maybe because you are now alone when before you had a partner, or because you have lost your job and need to find another, or because you have realised that your life or career is unsatisfactory.

You may feel you have no choice in what you do, but if you allow yourself to look for them the choices are there. You may be afraid to see them. Fear is a very important ingredient in depression, especially fear of change. When it comes to facing up to yourself, you prefer to carry on in the apparent security of an unchanging way of life because it is something you know, rather than changing how you live and work and feel for the better.

Overcoming this sort of fear is the positive way to get out of the dumps. You have so much potential. You can do so many different things, but up to now you probably haven't because you didn't want to take the risk or, even more important, you didn't want to make the choice, to take the decision.

In theory, the best time to get the most out of yourself would seem to be when all is going well – but life doesn't often work like this. When all is going smoothly very few of us stop and think about improvements. We are just grateful for the peace and calm of an undisturbed existence. So it is only when life goes out of kilter that we have the chance to change – and it is a chance that must be taken.

Why not take a few moments to look back over the past years? Remember all the plans and ambitions you had when you were much younger? What happened to them? Were they swept aside by marriage and family, by the fact that you gave up too soon, by impatience?

Whatever the reasons, write them down and also write down those early aspirations. Maybe amongst them there is something you could start again now.

And don't be put off if doing this makes you realise you've been travelling in the wrong direction for years. Maybe you did make a mistake and that is a blow, because you don't like to feel you've been that wrong about the way you're living your life – who does? But thinking like that will stop you changing – you'll always be hoping that things will work out. It takes courage to cut your losses and start again, whether it is in a job, a career, a relationship or just generally, but when you have done it the feeling of satisfaction and pride in yourself will be a terrific reward.

It will take you time to think things out, and if you instinctively feel, right at the start, that you may have made a mistake it does no harm to give yourself time to work out how best to improve your life. In the meantime, you can help yourself along in various ways.

If your main feeling at the moment is one of stagnation, don't fling yourself into just one major subject. Have fun. Dabble in all sorts of areas that interest you, be creative. Whether it is books you have always meant to read but never made the time for, a skill you have always wanted to acquire, an experience you've always put off having, get down to it now.

If your job is getting you down, plan to change – not immediately but in the near future. Give yourself time to think out whether you want to do something totally different or just slightly different but in the same field, and while you are deciding, start reading advertisements for jobs so that you can see what's available.

Maybe you would love to change your career or job but financially it is out of the question. In this case, you must make the very most of all the time you spend away from your job, so that although part of your life may be unsatisfying, at least it can be balanced by being very full and creative the rest of the time.

If your job simply doesn't stretch your mind, you can take advantage of the enormous variety of part-time courses available. There are local authority evening and day classes, extra-mural degree courses for those who didn't get to university but have some academic qualifications, the Open University which will give you the chance of a degree even if you've never been near an official exam paper, correspondence colleges which will see you through basic O- and A-level exams. The Government operates a variety of schemes where you can train or retrain for a new skill.

And if all you know at the moment is that you are in the wrong job you can go for careers advice at your local Job-Centre (free) or pay for a detailed consultation and tests at a careers advice centre.

These are all practical ways in which you can help your mind get through the depression which has attacked it.

Once you begin to feel a little stronger you can make use of this time in your life to get to know yourself better. Think about yourself – not just your faults but your qualities too. Get out of the habit of blaming yourself for things going wrong or, worse, always saying you couldn't help it, it just happened. You are responsible for the quality of your life, and you can make sure that your life is a good one.

You may have got into the terrible habit of not thinking very highly of yourself, of doing yourself down all the time. Realise that by doing this you are ill-treating yourself, and that you deserve better than that.

Now is the time to start being very self-centred, by thinking about yourself and your needs first. If you can get into the good habit of caring for yourself, you will find it much easier to care for others – and other people, far from resenting your behaviour, will see the strength it brings you, and that strength will benefit them too.

4

Pamper Your Body

Depression doesn't only affect your mind and your health, it affects your outward appearance too, and how you feel about the way you look.

Time and a gradual return to a peaceful state of mind will take away most of the marks of unhappiness but, in the meantime, what about today? Today you feel a mess, your eyes are strained with tension and weeping, your forehead creased with worry, your complexion grey with misery, and your whole body a mass of unidentifiable aches and pains.

If you've had a go at comforting your mind you can now turn your attention to your body, because it too needs comfort. Some people are already very aware of their bodies. They've been at it for years, smoothing in the creams and lotions, glorying in the luxury of a regular massage, treating themselves to a weekly sauna or facial. If you are among them, keep going because you really need it now.

But if, like most of us, you've never bothered with that sort of indulgence, now is the time to change your attitude. What you'll be aiming for is to give your body as much attention as you give your mind, never forgetting that if your body feels pampered and cared for it can also affect the way you feel about yourself in general.

The most important aim here is to reawaken you to the joy of touch. Touching is one of the most vital of our five senses. When we are small we are touched frequently by our parents and others who care for us but as we grow older touching, like crying, becomes less and less acceptable. You may find that the only time you touch and are touched is when you are in bed with your partner, and even then it may be cursory.

But people crave to be touched. It shows someone cares, it is contact between them and others, it can dull loneliness. Touching yourself can make you more aware and appreciative of your body.

So if you're worried that you'll be turning your bedroom or bathroom into some sort of beauty parlour, don't be – you won't. You'll just be looking after yourself. Anything goes now provided the end result makes you feel better. Choose whatever is right for you.

Bathe Your Cares Away

Baths have been popular for centuries as a way of relaxing, cleansing and perfuming the body. Even lying in a bath of plain warm water with no oils or salts in it is a soothing experience, but to get the most out of a bath you need to approach it in a slightly different way.

First, make sure your bathroom is conducive to relaxation. If you have only bright lights in there change the bulbs to a lower wattage or use candles.

The best time for a soothing bath is at night, but any time is right if it's right for you.

Don't have the water too hot. A hot bath is not good for you and could make you feel faint if you sit in it for too long.

What goes in the bath, apart from yourself? You can use any oil, essence, herb or salt you fancy. Choose something that softens hard water and has a pleasant fragrance, and avoid cheap salts with a very strong overpowering perfume.

What to do in the bath. That's up to you – whatever makes you feel most relaxed! If you are the type who normally hates to lie in a bath for longer than a few minutes, take in a good book or a radio to help the time pass quietly. Otherwise you can lie back, close your eyes and meditate.

The point is that if you want a bath to comfort you you must not rush it. Allow half an hour from start to finish. And if you are not alone in the house make sure you give strict instructions that you are not to be disturbed.

After the Bath

This is just as important as the bath itself. If all the towels you possess are ten years old, threadbare and just big enough to go round your waist and reach your knees, treat yourself to a brand new, fluffy, full-size bath sheet to cuddle in.

If the room is warm enough when you get out of the bath don't wrap up in a towel straightaway. Spread it out on the floor and lie down on it to let yourself dry slowly. If the room isn't warm enough, cuddle slowly into your new bath towel. If it's daytime get dressed slowly in clean clothes, not the ones you flung off before getting into the bath. Make a conscious effort to move slowly and deliberately. This is your time for yourself, so use it to the full, and that means up until the moment you open the bathroom door and step outside.

If your skin feels dry you can massage it with a little oil. Be careful not to overdo it – a little goes a very long way, and you don't want to emerge looking like a contestant for the Mr Universe competition.

Foot Baths

Your feet are not just for standing on, they are believed to contain control elements for many parts of your body, so a foot bath can actually make you feel good all over.

Simply put herbs or oils into a bowl of hot water, just as you would in a bath. Remember to use a muslin bag for herbs otherwise you'll spend hours picking bits out from between your toes. Sit quietly for about five or ten minutes, reading or meditating. Again, make sure you are alone, and don't think too much about what you look like; come to terms with the fact that people with their feet in water do look bizarre. Think instead of the good it's doing you. The best herbs to use are rosemary, peppermint, sage.

Massage Your Cares Away

Massage is one of the oldest therapies around. Administered in the right way, by an expert, it can cure and heal, but its main advantage if you are feeling fragile and hurt is that it makes you feel pampered. If you feel unloved and unlovable, rejected and despised, then to have someone touching you gently but firmly helps you to remember that you are worth something.

If you can afford it, splash out on a course of massages – say, once a week for six weeks. This will cost a lot but it is money well spent if the result is a more relaxed, less tense person. Even treating yourself to just one professional massage is worthwhile because it will give you a good idea of what massage is all about if you've never had one, and you'll know how you might be able to adapt it for yourself.

If you are prepared to pay for a very special sort of massage – and, after all, you deserve something out of the ordinary when you are depressed – you can try aromatherapy, in which the essential oils used for the treatment are adapted to suit the condition and personality of the individual. But be careful because there are only a few places that offer true aromatherapy treatments; many ordinary beauty salons offer something similar, but it is not the same.

A proper session should start with a longish discussion about your health, diet and lifestyle. Based on your answers the therapist will then mix the right oils for you. The actual session should last at least fifty minutes and the massage is slow and gentle, never violent or painful. Afterwards, if you've been to an expert, you should really feel almost as if you've been away for a weekend holiday – relaxed and tension-free.

The next best thing to a professional massage is a massage performed by someone who loves you. More about this in chapter 9 but, for the moment, if you can persuade a friend or partner simply to massage your neck and shoulders with a few drops of oil once in a while you will realise how soothing it is.

If there isn't anyone around who is close enough or caring enough to massage you, or if you are too shy to ask, you will have to go it alone. This doesn't negate the original comfort of massage – by massaging yourself, touching your body, you are showing your own respect and love for it. Obviously some areas, like the middle of your back, will be inaccessible, but you will gain comfort from what you can manage. Remember, above all, not to strain to reach all over, and to massage only for short periods so that your hands and arms don't get tired.

How to massage

Start off with your feet; in fact, a foot massage can stand on its own, as it were, although ideally someone else should do it for you. The therapy of foot massage, reflexology, claims to be able to pinpoint areas of your body which are not functioning properly, and help to cure them by massage. But your aim now is comfort and by massaging your feet you will be helping the rest of your body to relax without even touching it.

28

You will need oil or cream for this and it is ideal to do it after a bath or a foot bath. Start by kneading the sole of one foot and extend this to include the whole foot. Then concentrate on the ankle area and from there move on to massage each individual toe. Lie back on the floor, in the bath or wherever you happen to be to relax, as you will find it quite a strain reaching down for several minutes at a time unless you happen to be very supple or to have short legs. Then massage the other foot. You can do the same on your legs, rubbing in oil or lotion gently and firmly, and working up to your stomach, breasts/chest, and then down your arms, finishing with the fingers. Finally, attack the parts of your back which you can reach, along the top of the shoulders, which is in fact the area where the most tension collects. Feel gently with your fingers to find the knotted areas where you are really tense and gently massage them, working down into the knot with your fingers. You will also be able to reach the base of your spine; use both hands and push your fingers up as far as you can, without straining, on either side of the spine and then down again. Do this several times.

Putting a Face On It

Your face and head are the places where any strain or unhappiness will start to show and to be felt. You may feel as if a steel band is round your forehead, you may get headaches, aching eyes, even an aching jaw from clenching your teeth, and of course an aching neck. All this discomfort needs soothing away and it is worth spending time on this.

Facials and masks have always been traditionally thought of as feminine pursuits, probably because they are invariably associated with beautifying a woman's looks. At the moment you are not after a more beautiful face, you want a relaxed face, a comforted face, so there's no need for men to feel effeminate or women to feel too beauty-conscious about using some of the following ideas. Remember *anything* goes now, as long as it makes you feel better.

If you can afford to have a facial in a salon so much the better because the massage is especially beneficial if it is professionally done, but it is possible to give yourself a facial at home and get more or less the same soothing effect, using essential oils or a light cream and gently rubbing this into your face and neck.

Other Tips

Your eyes. They'll be feeling under the weather at the moment, either strained from the tension within or red from tears or dark-ringed from lack of sleep or a bad diet. Go back to the old-fashioned remedies of placing slices of uncooked potato or cucumber over them for 10 minutes and just lying quietly. Damp tea bags are good too and so is a little witch hazel on a couple of cotton wool pads.

Your hands. Look after them in the same way as your feet, bathing them in warm water with herbs or oils. Rub in cream, making the massage calm and soothing.

Your hair. Having your hair done is soothing and can cheer up your mood. But don't get carried away. If you've always had long flowing locks now is probably not the right time to have an Eton crop. If you are a man, however, it might be a good time to grow a beard and avoid the daily drudge of shaving. But just going to the hairdresser for a trim, wash and blow dry is a good idea. Having your hair washed is probably the best part of the session and you get in a good scalp massage too, although you can do this for yourself at home quite effectively. It's another excellent way of curing tension headaches.

You might like to experiment with hair colouring, too – highlights are not too drastic, or you can go for the semi-permanent colours that wash out after a few times.

Try to massage your scalp every day, starting at the nape of your neck and working up and forward to your forehead.

Pampering Away From Home

One way of solving a lone holiday problem is to stay on a health farm for a few days. It's an expensive holiday, but that does include three meals a day, which makes it good value unless you are on a strict diet, in which case it's a lot to pay for lettuce leaves and halves of grapefruit. It also includes several treatments each day, such as a sauna, steam baths, massage, and seaweed baths. Some places have swimming pools and most have good grounds where you can play tennis, croquet, or just walk. Other treatments like manicures, pedicures and facials are usually extra.

The nice thing about these places is that nowadays people go to them not just because they want to lose weight but because they desperately need to relax, rest, calm down. So the atmosphere is usually friendly and the people, despite the high cost, aren't necessarily particularly wealthy. Mostly they're just average people who choose to spend some money in this particular way.

Another alternative is the one mentioned earlier – a course of treatments at a beauty or health salon. A series of facials or massages booked ahead will give you something to look forward to as well as making you feel pampered. Some health farms are also open for day visitors. You can spend a whole day being pampered, wandering from sauna to jacuzzi and so on.

5

Eating and Enjoying Your Food

Food is very low down on your list of priorities right now. The mere thought of sitting down to a meal or, worse still, having to prepare one, is enough to kill your meagre appetite. Maybe you don't bother to eat, struggling through the day on cigarettes and endless cups of coffee.

On the other hand, you could be one of those people who head straight for the fridge or larder the minute they feel down. Your day is spent eating vast amounts of filling foods – you eat even if you are not particularly hungry, hoping that feeling full will dull the pain. Or you go to extremes and eat nothing all day, but find yourself in the kitchen at two in the morning cooking bacon sandwiches.

Eating too little or too much is not going to help to make you feel less depressed – in fact, it will do just the opposite. If you virtually starve yourself you will feel more tired and listless. You could even end up being physically ill. Overeating will make you uncomfortable and fat. Every time you look in the mirror and see your pasty face and obese body you will hate yourself. And if your depression has been triggered off by weight problems you will feel even worse and it will be harder to control your urge to stuff.

First, recognise how useful food is. The right food eaten in the right amounts will give you energy and keep you healthy, and you need both these things now. Food can also be a great comforter. Think back to your childhood and remember how a meal or a particular food could often make you feel so much better.

But before you decide *what* you are going to eat, you need to cope with the problem of *how*.

If You've Lost Your Appetite

Eating very little is an easy trap to fall into. It happens without you even being aware of it. You'll start off the day by skipping breakfast, and then lunch and by the time evening comes you are too tired to bother.

Without enough food to stimulate your taste buds your appetite decreases. If you are not careful, and if there is no one around to encourage you, you could soon reach the stage of having to force yourself to eat.

This is even more likely to happen if you are worried about being overweight. You may think you are doing yourself a favour, that days without food will stop you from getting fat. You'll be slim, lithe, attractive. But you are deluding yourself. In the end, however slim you really are, and the scales tell you you are, you won't admit it. When you look at yourself you'll still want to lose a few more pounds. Then you will be well on the way to becoming anorexic and when that happens only specialist treatment can help you.

But at the moment you *can* help yourself.

Sit down and make a list of all your favourite foods. Balance the list so that you have equal amounts of sweet and savoury. Pick an item from each section and aim to eat them *today*. Do the same the next day and so on for a week until your appetite has been restored.

If you are the person who always does the cooking, persuade someone else to take over a while, even if it is only for one meal a day. You are likely to have a better appetite for a meal that you haven't had to prepare.

If you are alone with children you can either let the older ones take over the occasional meal, or at least make sure that you sit down and eat with them.

If you are completely alone you will find it hardest of all because it will mean cooking a solitary meal, and it is at this point that many people stop eating.

Get round the problem by making the main meal of the day a special occasion. Don't eat on your knees in front of the television. Lay the table properly. Light candles. Experiment with recipes you haven't tried before.

If You Are Over-Eating

This is a hard habit to kick at the best of times, and now it will be even harder. The trouble with food is that it is always around.

If you don't work and are at home all day, you'll have cupboards full of food and visits to the shops to tempt you. If you go to work, there are restaurants, cafés, the canteen, the pub.

Obviously now is not the time to go on a strict diet, unless you are very strong willed. But you can make small steps in the right direction.

Over the next week write down all the food you eat each day. Put a red ring around those foods you know are fattening and sweet and a blue ring round those that are fattening and savoury. The following week, aim to eat only one of the ringed sweet items on your list but don't worry too much about the savoury foods. It is far better to indulge in a huge steak with a pile of mashed potatoes than six sticky buns.

Next time you are tempted to raid the food cupboard for a handful of biscuits, spend half an hour doing something else – reading, watching television, going for a walk.

Only eat when you feel really hungry. If you get struck by terrible hunger pangs between meals make sure you have a variety of raw foods around. Fill the fridge with carrot and celery sticks and keep a good supply of fresh fruit within easy reach.

The next stage is to plan a diet of the foods that are best for you.

When you start to think about what to eat you need to bear two factors in mind. Firstly, the food you eat needs to be good for you, because you want it to make you healthy and give you strength and energy. At the same time, you want food to comfort you.

When you are depressed you are a little like a convalescent. You don't feel very strong either physically or mentally. The foods you crave are the simple foods – either simple to eat or simple to prepare – and you tend to go for bland flavours. Anything very highly spiced, such as curry, is just too much for your system to cope with.

Because depression can affect your body as well as your mind you need to look after your digestion. You may be getting butterflies in your stomach or a lot of indigestion, so the food you eat must be easy to digest.

Most people have their own 'comfort' food, which they turn to when they are feeling low. Usually it is something sweet – maybe as a child you were given chocolate or biscuits whenever you cried and the habit was formed then. Or, because as a baby the first food you experienced was sweet milk, you subconsciously long to return to those days of uncomplicated living and the comfort of the breast or bottle.

But sweet comfort foods cannot and must not be your whole diet. They are something you treat yourself to once in a while.

The secret of most comfort foods is that they need little or no preparation, so they can be there when you need them most. That is their advantage, and their drawback, too, if you don't want to get carried away.

If you have never really thought about what food comforts you most, here are a few ideas, all tried and tested and approved by people who have felt just as you do now.

Comfort Foods

Milk for comfort

It's really back to babyhood and childhood for these but they certainly work for some.

- Cereal and milk is comforting, especially porridge.
- Warm milk with brown sugar or honey is a soothing way to end the day.
- Rice, tapioca or sago pudding – you either love them or loathe them.
- Custard, either on its own or over fruit.

The sweet comforters

These are mostly full of what nutritionists call 'empty calories', but you deserve them once in a while.

- Chocolate.
- Chewing gum.
- Barley sugar.
- Toffee and fudge.
- Biscuits.
- Cakes, with or without cream.
- Buns, the stickier the better.
- Candy floss.
- Toffee apples.

- Dolly mixtures.
- Liquorice allsorts.
- Jelly babies.
- Smarties.
- Ice cream.

The savoury comforters

Most of these are good for you, as well as bringing back childhood memories. Substitute low-fat margarine for butter if you are worried about your cholesterol levels.

- Freshly mashed potato with butter and pepper.
- Spaghetti with melted butter.
- Scambled or poached egg on toast.
- Lightly boiled egg with bread soldiers.
- Creamed mushrooms on toast.
- Bacon sandwiches.
- Fried tomatoes on fried bread – some people like to sprinkle sugar on too.
- Smoked salmon.
- Caviare.
- Lobster.
- Bread and butter, toast and butter or crumpets or croissants.
- Spinach.
- Fish fingers.
- Avocado pear.
- Strawberries – only fresh ones will do, with or without cream and sugar.
- Peaches, pears and very fresh apples.
- Mangoes.
- Jerusalem artichokes, mashed with plenty of butter.
- Mashed banana and cream.
- Babies' rusks.
- Cheese on toast.
- Bread and butter with cream cheese and strawberry jam, or with sugar.
- Liver paté.

Nearly all of these foods need very little preparation, but don't forget that comfort can come from cooking. It can be very soothing to stand by the stove stirring a creamy sauce or to sit in the kitchen with a book while delicious smells waft their way across the room.

When you cook keep the preparation simple. Don't, unless you really feel in the mood, go for elaborate recipes that require hours of cutting, stirring, cooking. It will be too exhausting and you want to expend the minimum of effort and get the maximum enjoyment out of actually eating.

Drinking Your Cares Away

It's all too easy to head for the pub or reach for the whisky bottle when life is getting you down, as if they could be the answer to your problems.

Of course they will dull the pain for a while, but you'll only end up with a hangover and you could find yourself drinking more and more as time goes by.

An alcoholic drink in the right quantities and at the right time is fine. You can quite justifiably treat yourself to a pre-lunch drink, but have it when you are sitting down quietly. You can do the same in the evening, after work or before a meal, but don't get into the habit at the moment of carrying a glass around with you when you are cooking.

You may also find yourself drinking coffee and tea in ever greater quantities, because their caffeine and tannin content pep you up a bit. They help to keep you awake at night, too, if that's what you want. But they aren't good for you, and their main content is water – you can do better than that.

Much more comforting are liquids that *are* good for you – apple juice, orange juice or grape juice, for example. If you have a juice extractor you can concoct all sorts of drinks from vegetables and fruit, mixing and tasting until you find the ones you like.

You can make delicious milk shakes in a liquidiser, using real fruit instead of artificial additives.

Herbal teas are very comforting, too, although they do take a bit of getting used to, especially if you take sugar in your tea or coffee. Try camomile, lime blossom (tilleul), rose hip, mint. You can get these in convenient sachets from health food stores. Other herbal teas or infusions can lift depression: borage was called by Bacon 'A soverreign drink for melancholy passion' and lemon balm leaves are supposed to have a similar effect, as are thyme and sage. To prepare, pour 25 cl (½ pt) boiling water over a teaspoon of leaves and let it stand for 2 or 3 minutes.

6

Exercise for Comfort

It sounds like a real contradiction in terms, doesn't it? How can exercise be equated with any sort of comfort? But it can be, and as the comfort it provides can actually end up being good for you too, that's an extra bonus.

First of all, although it may seem hard to do so now, think about your health. If you are unhealthy and out of condition you may feel tired, not have much appetite, be overweight, have dull skin and eyes, sleep badly, be irritable and easily bored. The list is endless, and probably echoes the way you feel when you are depressed as well. That's because the connection between mind and body is very close indeed, and if one is out of condition it affects the other.

You already have a lot on your plate as far as your mind is concerned. It's a struggle to get through each day. The wonderful thing about exercise is that it helps take the strain off your mind and at the same time gives you an excellent chance of feeling better physically and mentally.

Bear in mind that exercise, done in the right way, can benefit every part of your body. Exercise means movement, movement means using your muscles. Muscles need oxygen to function properly which means that your circulation system, the blood which carries the oxygen to all parts of the body as well as the muscles, will work more efficiently. Result: a fitter, healthier you.

Maybe the thought of struggling and straining to get fit makes you groan and want to hide in the nearest armchair. But it really isn't as bad as all that, provided you bear a couple of points in mind. First, you won't get fit overnight, especially if you haven't exercised for years. So don't expect miracles – fitness will come gradually but surely, provided you stick at it and don't give up. Secondly, don't overdo it. If you are over thirty and haven't exercised for years have a check up with your doctor before you embark on any form of exercise. Start slowly and you'll be amazed at how quickly you can work your way up to doing more than you ever imagined, but without pain or strain.

If you are feeling particularly lethargic and anti-exercise at the moment you may well be wondering what on earth the benefits can possibly be, and whether it's worth making the effort. If you have always been an unsporty type, who invariably tried to get out of games at school, you are going to find it hard to make even a small start. Just remember that although some people may be better at some games than the rest of us, we are all equipped to do some form of exercise. Our bodies have changed very little since the days of primitive cave dwellers fighting and hunting for survival. What *has* changed for most of us is the ability to use our bodies properly so that many muscles are lying inactive and flabby.

But you are looking for comfort and surprisingly that is just what exercise can offer, in three different ways. First, it gives you something to do, something that will fill your mind. If your depression is caused by the end of a relationship, for instance, you need something to fill the empty hours. Also, you will find it quite hard to think about your problems when all your energies are concentrated on chasing a ball round a squash court, trying to make it to the end of the swimming bath before you drown or jogging round the block.

Second, and more subtly, by setting yourself some sort of exercise target, and sticking to it, you will begin to feel proud of yourself again, and of your achievement, especially if you have taken the trouble to organise a daily schedule and have kept to it. At the moment your self-respect level is at an all-time low, so anything you do to raise it up can't be bad.

Finally, exercise taken regularly over a period of, say, six weeks will make you feel and look better. You may find it easier to sleep, be less irritable, lose some weight. Your skin and eyes will begin to look fresher and brighter. In other words, a new improved you will emerge. Even if you don't exercise every single day, each time you do some exercise, without straining, you will feel just that bit fitter, and it will help you feel calmer in your mind as well.

A couple of drawbacks. Your problem is going to be getting started and keeping at it. If you can make it through the first two weeks you'll be over the worst, but your feeling at present is probably that it's bad enough having to get up and cope with a normal day, let alone one including an exercise schedule. But it is worth trying, whatever your initial feelings. If it doesn't suit you then give it up and go on to something else. Better still, give exercise as a whole a try and work your way though the various types. Maybe on the way you will find one that is perfect for your personality and mood, and if you don't you'll have spent a few weeks improving your health anyway, so you won't lose out.

The other drawback will come from other people. Physical exercise is 'in' at the moment. It's been heavily promoted all over the place; whole books and complete television series are devoted to the subject. The trouble is that promoting one way of life makes those living differently even more adamant that they are not going to follow it. So you are going to have to prove to yourself that it makes you feel better. Don't just go by what other people tell you, either for or against. Like sex, you've got to try it for yourself, before you can realise how good it is.

Getting Started

Make a plan of action. Sit down and decide how much time you can spare *regularly* for exercise. If you can settle on the same time each day it will be easier to keep to, and will enable other people in your life to adapt to it too. Maybe you think you have too little time. Most people have very little time, but if you can put aside five minutes a day to start with, you'll be on the right track.

Knowing the type of person you are you can also decide what time of day suits you best. If you are good at getting up in the morning then rising a little earlier to fit in exercise isn't going to be too traumatic. If, on the other hand, you only come alive at night, plan to exercise in the early evening or last thing at night.

What sort of exercise?

Making a schedule will automatically limit the possibilities. For instance, you may want to swim but if the baths are a long way away and you can only get there once a week it will be best to treat this as an extra exercise. Try to choose something that will fit in with your life because then it's easier to keep going.

To help you get started almost without realising it there are a few things you can slot into your life without buying a single item of clothing or equipment.

Walking. Walk somewhere each day where you previously used car, bus or train – but don't meander, walk briskly.

Stairs. Use stairs instead of escalator or lift whenever you can, for going up and for coming down. You can try your first exercise in stair running, too, for which you need a flight of about eight or ten steps. Start by going up and down briskly three times and increase the amount each day or so, provided you don't get puffed. If you do get out of breath, stick at the same level for a little longer.

Buy a skipping rope. You probably haven't used one for years but skipping is one of those once-learned, never forgotten skills like riding a bike or swimming. It may be a bit tricky to start with but you'll soon get the hang of it again. Start off with ten skips, and increase by five each day.

An Indoor Exercise Routine

If you think that you might be put off by bad weather conditions follow a pattern of exercises indoors. You can start with just two or three exercises and build up from there. The advantage of doing it this way, instead of going through the dozen or so most exercise and health books recommend, is that they take up just a few minutes, and so are easy to fit in, especially if you are not in the mood. And you avoid all the business of looking up and trying to remember about ten different exercises when your mind is not working efficiently.

Getting ready

You need space and a room that is warm but not hot and stuffy. An open window, provided there isn't a howling gale outside, is a good idea. The floor should be carpeted, or you can use a mat, a blanket doubled over, or a large piece of foam.

What to wear – as little as possible is the answer to that one. A leotard is comfortable, plus tights and leg warmers for cold weather, but make sure the tights are footless and your feet are bare. For men, shorts and a T-shirt.

Before you start. Make sure you won't be disturbed or interrupted. If you have time, lie on the floor and relax first. This is important if you are doing exercises in the evening after a hard day at work. In the morning, if you are rushed, six deep breaths at the window is a good alternative, provided the air around you is safe to breathe!

The basic three exercises

1. Standing straight with legs about 23 cm (9 in) apart, or whatever is most comfortable, do arm circling. Start with your arms by your sides, then raise them together forwards and up until they are over your head, then drop them down sideways until they are back where you started. That's all. You should feel a pull as your arms go down past your head and back to the starting position. Repeat this ten times to start with and as you get more supple you can increase this to fifteen and then twenty times.

2. Stand as before, with hands by your sides. This time, bend forward from the waist, letting your hands and arms hang absolutely free and relaxed as you do so. Bend as far as you can without falling flat on your face and bounce up and down four times. Slowly straighten up again. Then arch your back backwards, let your head and neck drop back, keeping your arms relaxed at your sides. Bounce four times and return to the upright position. Repeat twice to start with and increase up to five times. That's all there is to it, except that as you get better you can stand with your feet closer together and you'll also find, gradually and amazingly, that your hands will get closer and closer to touching the floor, but don't strain to do this at the start.

3. For this final exercise you will actually need a piece of equipment – a wall. Stand with your feet together, facing the wall and at arm's length from it. Place your hands, palms downwards, on the wall. Bend slowly at the elbows so that you fall in towards the wall. Just before you smash your face in, stop and push back out again. There you are doing press-ups! Do this five times to start with and increase over the weeks to ten, twenty and eventually thirty.

If you think you can cope with one final exercise at this stage you can end the session by running gently on the spot for 30 seconds.

Exercising Out of Doors

If you prefer to exercise out of doors, there are several activities to choose from. If you are on a basic fitness programme you want to steer clear of competitive sports that provide exercise at this stage. Though these give you a social life, too often the exercise they provide is very disjointed – you rush around madly for a few minutes, then stop, rush again, then stop, which is not the sort of activity to make your physical organs feel comforted. So go for a more steady form of outside exercise. Three good possibilities are jogging, cycling and swimming. You may be able to think of others too.

Jogging

This is probably the easiest way to get fit out of doors with the minimum of effort and training. You don't have to have a special skill to be able to jog provided you know how to walk, though even that's an activity some people are fast forgetting.

As with all activities, if you haven't done anything for years, don't go mad now and rush off on a mile jog round the block. Remember you are supposed to be pampering yourself, not putting yourself through a third-degree torture.

The main purpose of jogging is to improve the way your heart, lungs and circulatory system work. By getting more blood pumping round your system, the whole system and organs will work more efficiently. The advantage of jogging is that it is rhythmical, and it is also non-competitive. If you do jog with a friend keep to your own pace all the time – never strain to overtake or keep up. The other benefit you may get from jogging is peace of mind – many dedicated joggers claim this happens after a while.

Before you start

If you are over thirty and haven't done exercise for more than a year and/or are overweight, check with your doctor before you start any jogging. Have the right clothes for the jog. The most important item is footwear. It's worth getting decent shoes – you don't *have* to buy running shoes but a pair of well-made tennis shoes or trainers are perfect and give a slight bounce to your stride. Apart from that, anything goes as long as it's comfortable: shorts and T-shirt in summer and, in winter, loose trousers, a T-shirt to soak up the sweat with a pullover or track suit top over it for warmth. If it's really cold wear gloves as well; being cold is pointless and will make you tense.

Where to jog

Nearly all the books on jogging cheerfully tell you to jog anywhere. Just walk out of your front door, they say, and jog off down the street. It doesn't matter if there's traffic around or the pavements are crowded, doing the jogging is what counts.

But in your present mood jogging down a crowded city street may not be particularly enjoyable. And who wants to inhale all those fumes if they can avoid them?

So if you have a car or a convenient bus service, use this to go to your nearest open space, park, beach or whatever and do your jogging there in peace and surrounded by natural beauty and fresh, reasonably unpolluted air. The only danger to this method is that it's easier not to bother to jog if you have to go somewhere else first. You know yourself best, your weakness or strength of character and if you *know* that you'll only keep it up if you do it more or less out of your own front door, ignore the drawbacks of the surroundings and do just that.

If you want to get fit it's much better to choose one activity to start with and stick to it. So if jogging is your choice you should jog every day or every other day. Time of day is irrelevant but don't go immediately after a meal. You'll need to allow about ten to fifteen minutes per day.

How to start

As with everything else, slowly. In fact, the best way to start is to spend the first three days just walking – but not wandering along, walking briskly, holding yourself up and swinging your arms and breathing deeply in and out as you do so. Then gradually introduce some jogging into your walk each day. Jog for a minute, walk for three minutes, then jog again and so on. Increase the amount of jogging until you feel comfortable. You should never be out of breath, puffed or unable to talk when you return. Until you can jog comfortably for ten consecutive minutes always end the session with a five minute walk.

Remember you are supposed to be enjoying yourself, so don't make it into a terrible strain. As you walk or jog round the streets or through the park, let your mind relax into a form of meditation, concentrating on the physical aspects of what you are doing, your breathing or on what is going on round you.

Jogging doesn't suit everyone – if you find it a bore or a slog then give it up and try something else.

Cycling

The wonderful thing about cycling is that added height it gives you as you travel along, so that you can get an entirely new perspective on familiar sights. As well as that, you are moving at a good speed for some of the time and exercising your legs, feet, ankles, shoulders, back and stomach muscles, so it's certainly pretty healthy.

The big drawback is that it is also dangerous these days. In fact, if you live in town don't use cycling as exercise and certainly not as a comfort exercise – the stress and strain of coping with traffic will undo any physical benefit. But if you live away from heavy traffic, it's a good exercise to do regularly each day for about fifteen minutes. Don't use the same route all the time as you'll get bored.

If you need to buy a bike make sure you get decent advice on the right size and type for you. You need a model with gears. It's pointless having a machine that puts a strain on your back or legs because it's the wrong size and if you really plan to cycle regularly then it's worth spending the extra on a good model.

Swimming

If you have a pool near enough to get to easily each day, this is an ideal exercise. Swimming a variety of strokes like crawl, breast-stroke and backstroke will exercise virtually every area of your body.

Start off with no more than ten minutes in the water. You will be busy for all of that time so it's not really a waste of the entrance ticket. If you can do these three strokes devote a minute to each to start with. So swim for three minutes and then have a break. Build this up to two minutes, then three, four and eventually five per stroke, but spread it over weeks rather than days and only do as much as is comfortable.

If it's difficult to get to the pool every day see if you can manage three days. This is enough, if kept up regularly, to get you pretty fit. Try and pick a time when the pool is uncrowded otherwise you'll find it hard to get a good rhythm going.

Always shower off afterwards otherwise you'll spend the rest of the day smelling like a swimming pool and not feel at all refreshed.

Yoga

If you are mixed up, don't know which way to turn, depressed and, on top of it all, unfit and tense, then yoga may be a perfect answer. At its most simplistic the variation of yoga we know best, hatha yoga, is a combination of exercises in breathing, posture and movement plus a mind exerciser – it is possible to become far more self-aware through yoga. It is so popular now that there are plenty of classes available both in the evening and during the day so, if you prefer to be taught, rather than learning from a book, you won't have much difficulty in arranging that.

What you may miss out on, unless you are lucky enough to have a very experienced teacher, is the inner depths of yoga. All sorts of people now teach yoga because they can do the positions – physiotherapists, and dance teachers, who are supple anyway, for example – but frequently all they will teach you are the movements. The extra mind-expanding, meditative qualities that yoga can provide will only come if you happen to light on a genuine yoga teacher with whom you are in tune.

But, don't despair, you can at least benefit from the postures, or asanas, as they are called. And, like jogging, yoga is non-competitive. You do the best you can and, with practice, you improve all the time. No one expects you to twist yourself into knots straightaway and do yourself a major injury.

47

Before you start

Whether you do yoga at home or in a class you need the right clothes – a leotard or shorts and T-shirt are best. Don't wear anything on your feet. At home you need a room with a hard floor but have a mat at least 2.5 cm (1 in) thick or a blanket folded double to protect your back and neck during some of the asanas. Make sure you aren't going to be disturbed, take the phone off the hook, muzzle the door bell and the dog.

Competitive Sport

At the moment certain kinds of exercise are perfect for you – but only if you are reasonably fit and supple to start with. And they certainly need not be thought of as a plan to get fit, because just doing them occasionally can make you feel a whole lot better.

If you've got a lot of aggression in you and no outlet for it then a hard, fast game of tennis, squash or badminton, may help. All that rushing around, bashing a ball over a net or at a wall, getting physically exhausted and having to concentrate hard for half an hour or so, will at the very least give you a break from what is on your mind. The same applies to team games like football, hockey, rugger, netball – in fact, any activity that demands total concentration over a short space of time. If you've been feeling very out of things as well then any team game will help you feel less alone.

7

Putting Your Money in its Place

Everyone worries about money at times. In fact, feeling depressed about money, or the lack of it, is as common an ailment as a cold and just as hard to get rid of if you let the mood get a hold on you.

Remember Mr Micawber? 'Annual income twenty pounds, annual expenditure nineteen pounds nineteen and six, result happiness. Annual income twenty pounds, annual expenditure twenty pounds and six, result misery.'

He was right. There is a very fine line to be drawn between living within your budget and more or less allowing your money to take a back seat, and the alternative when money takes over and starts to rule your life.

If you are going to read this chapter, do so bearing the following thought in mind. The money you have at the moment is yours, you have gone out to work and earned it, and that applies even if you are unemployed because you will be getting benefits you have paid for in the past.

So, it's your money and it has no right whatsoever to make your life a misery. When you spend it you should enjoy doing so. In the same way that you can control what you do with your life, so you should also be able to control your money and how it affects you. Promise yourself right now that you, and not your money, are going to be in charge.

There are two ways in which you can achieve this. Your aim is to get your money worries into perspective, and under your control, and this can be done both practically and, just as important, by altering your attitude towards money.

Working Out What You Owe

First, on a purely practical level, the more organised you are about money the better you will feel. The best way of regaining control is to spend some time finding out exactly where you stand. Don't be afraid that this will involve hours spent poring over sums, or that discovering the true state of your finances will make you feel even more depressed. In fact, this knowledge will give you power and strength.

At its simplest level, being organised about money means having a clear idea of your income and outgoings. Set aside an hour. Sit down at a cleared table with a blank sheet of paper divided into two. Gather round you beforehand all the bits and pieces that have to do with money: your bank statements, pay slips, building society books, post office savings book, cheque book, credit card statements, and so on. Include any recent major bills for services that you use regularly, such as rates, gas, electricity, and telephone.

On one side of the paper write down your income. Include any small payments apart from your regular job income; for instance, if you are a mother with children of school-age or under, don't forget family allowance payments.

On the opposite side of your paper write down all your outgoings. If you are paid weekly write down outgoings on a weekly basis even if some are only paid annually. If you are on a monthly salary, calculate on a monthly basis. Don't leave out such items as travel to and from work, car tax and insurance, newspaper bills. If you can't be totally accurate, it is best to over-estimate on what you might spend.

Then add up your two sets of figures, and see what the difference is between them.

If you have never done this exercise before it could turn out to be quite a revelation. But if the discrepancy between income and expenditure is large, don't panic or despair. Remind yourself that you are better off knowing where you stand because you are in a better position to do something about it.

If the shortfall between income and expenditure is a permanent one – in other words, if you are overdrawn to the same amount each month – put this amount into perspective. That is, if it is around £100 and you can earn around £5,000 a year, remember that that overdraft of £100 each month represents a tiny percentage of your total income over the year – around 2 per cent. Is it really worth losing sleep over such a small sum?

But if your overdraft or shortage of cash is a temporary aberration running into several hundreds something has clearly gone wrong, and your list will make it clear where the problem lies. But what are you going to do about it?

Now that you are organised on one level you can plan better on another. Some of your expenses cannot be avoided. Large quarterly bills for gas and electricity, for instance – you know they will come but you don't plan ahead for them. If you do so, they will hurt far less and, best of all, you will know where you stand with other outgoings.

Most consumer-type bills can be paid for by monthly instalments. If you are getting paid regularly it is worth setting aside a sum of money each month to spread the load.

If you have debts all over the place and, now that you see these written down in black and white, you feel desperate then you probably need expert advice.

How to Make Your Bank Manager into Your Best Friend

Most people regard their bank manager either as an unsympathetic ogre, only getting in touch when things look black (or rather red), or as a strict parent, ever eager to reprimand as they step out of line. So they try to pretend their bank manager doesn't exist, until things get to such a state that they can no longer ignore him. But your bank manager can help you sort out your problems – if he knows about them.

The next time you try to avoid your bank manager, remember this. If you have a current account with a bank you are a customer. You pay for the privilege of keeping your money in the bank but in return the bank gets to use your money. You are entitled to more service than just going in periodically to withdraw cash, and one of the best services a bank can offer is advice from the manager.

There are a few ground rules for getting the best from a bank manager. Observe them and it could solve a multitude of money problems.

Rule One – be honest. Think of him as a sort of doctor. A doctor can't begin to cure an illness unless you tell him the symptoms in some detail, although he can prescribe certain basic remedies based on observation of the patient. In the same way your bank manager will come up with basic remedies for your money situation – refusing to honour cheques, writing you stern letters and so on. But if you explain your problems in detail he may be able to come up with much less painful and more effective solutions.

Rule Two – try to make the first move. This is intelligent psychology. If you can, always approach your bank manager before he comes to you. If you know you are going to be overdrawn at the end of the month write and tell the bank. If you want to spend a large sum discuss it with him first.

Rule Three – be prepared to give plenty of information. Your bank manager can tell from the state of your account whether you are coping or not, but he's not telepathic. He can only work on the information available so the more you can tell him, not only about your income but about your home, your family, your prospects, the better he will understand and the more he'll be able to help.

What sort of help can you expect?

If those large quarterly and annual bills are getting you down, most banks can offer the facility of a budget account. You add together all your major regular bills and divide the total by twelve, and each month that amount is transferred into a special budget account. As and when the bills come in you pay them from this account (you will be issued with a separate cheque book for this). If you've done your calculations correctly you should end the year in balance, although there may be times when you are temporarily overdrawn. This way you know that certain major financial commitments are being dealt with, making it easier to cope with how you spend your remaining income.

If you have a large number of debts, your manager may suggest gathering them all together in one place in the form of a bank loan. Though this means a lump sum to pay off, at least you can pay off individual outstanding bills. Then each week or month you will have to set aside a sum to pay off your loan. Loans of this kind are not cheap and the knowledge that they exist may depress you, but one large debt is easier to control than several smaller ones. Try to make the pay-off period as short as possible. It may hurt to tighten your belt for a while but it will get everything over and done with much sooner.

Other Practical Ways to Cope

If you don't have a bank account and are paid weekly it is a good idea to put your money into the post office or a building society. As soon as you are paid set aside money for the weekly essentials, including contributions towards monthly or quarterly bills. Do the week's food shopping at once, too.

If you are the sort of person who loses things easily, treat yourself to some files. Get different colours if possible and mark each file clearly. Use a separate file for each item – electricity, gas, phone, income slips, and so on. Whenever a bill or payment advice comes in, file it at once.

Check all your outgoings carefully once a month. In these computerised times mistakes do occur and the only person likely to notice them is you. If you only get bank statements occasionally it is well worth organising monthly statements; it costs a little more but it is much easier to keep track of your cheques, standing orders, direct debits and so on.

If you own a credit card, check these outgoings too, as code numbers are easily mixed up. And if that credit card is becoming an expensive financial liability, destroy it – cut it up into tiny pieces and throw it in the dustbin so you won't be tempted. Don't worry, you'll be sent a new one when the old one would have expired, and by then you may be in a better position financially.

If you are unfortunate enough to be with a bank that insists on making its credit card double up as a cheque guarantee card, you obviously can't throw it away. But try not to take your cheque book or card with you all the time. Buy as much as you can with cash, limiting visits to the bank to once a week.

Incidentally, paying cash can often save money. And don't be afraid to ask for a discount for cash, which can be anything from 10 to 20 per cent off the bill.

Know your rights. If you are in rented accommodation you may qualify for a rebate if your rent goes up exorbitantly. The same applies to rates if you feel yours are higher than they should be. Never be afraid to ask – you have nothing to lose and a lot to gain.

Take greater care at home with the way you use services. Gas and electricity are expensive and it is very easy to be carelessly extravagant with them. Get into the habit of switching appliances off as you leave the room. If you really can't make ends meet, live in one room for a while; concentrating your resources into one space like the kitchen is more comfortable than turning down heating all over the house.

A phone is expensive, too, though it may be a comfort to you if you feel lonely and isolated. But if your depression is due to lack of cash then you are going to have to be tough with the way you use your phone. Get into the habit of monitoring the length of your calls and limit your conversation to basics. If possible, arrange for people to phone you and if you have to make a call try to avoid doing so during the day. All personal calls should be made in the evenings, if possible, and business calls at least in the afternoon when the rates are slightly cheaper.

If the person you have phoned needs to look something up, be tough and ask him to phone back. You can also save money on phone bills by phoning when you know a person you want to speak to isn't there, and leave a message for him to call back. If you are having to foot the bill for other people's calls as well, you can buy a simple lock to put on the phone. You can keep a check on how much gas or electricity you are using by having a pay-as-you-use meter installed, but this will cost you, of course, and you may feel the price too high for the return.

If Debts Have Built Up

There's nothing worse than the knowledge that you owe money to all and sundry, and that any moment now they are going to start demanding payment.

As with a bank manager, honesty is the best approach. Instead of pretending you haven't received demanding letters, or contemplating changing your name or emigrating, come clean. Write a letter to your creditors, explaining the situation and offering a constructive solution. This may be quite a simple matter. For example, in the case of hiring a television set you could terminate the agreement for a while, or you could offer to continue repayments at a lower level. The solution may be more complex, but the most important thing is to show willing. Remember, no company is going to grind you into the ground if you have no capital worth having. If you show that you are prepared to do your best and that you are not deliberately avoiding payment, you will be in a much stronger position if the worst comes to the worst and the creditor decides to sue you. The law is not inevitably on the side of the creditor; if you are in bad financial circumstances you can get the advice of a lawyer via legal aid.

Some people can't resist entering into hire purchase agreements, and often it does make sense to buy now rather than later. But if you are short of cash try to resist the temptation.

If you are unemployed you have to cope with the emotional trauma of feeling unwanted as well as a reduced income. On the practical side, make the most of any reduncancy money you receive – you may feel it should all be saved but if you have been given a large sum you should certainly not feel at all guilty about spending some of it on a really good holiday or new furniture.

Make sure, too, that you are receiving all the State benefits you are entitled to. Quite often you will not be told about extra benefits, so it is very much in your own interests to find out as much as you can.

Think about ways of making extra money, but weigh up very carefully whether it is worth while. There is more to life than earning money – the quality of your life is just as important. Moonlighting, for instance, may earn you extra cash but will the price be too high? Will your family lose out or will you be too exhausted to enjoy other things in life?

Start Saving

The idea may seem preposterous right now and for a while you may only be able to save in a rather negative way, by cutting down on some of the things you normally buy. But, as you straighten your budget out, remember that if you can save just £2 a week, by the end of the year you will have over £100 put aside. If you put the money in a savings account obviously it will earn interest.

The Emotional Aspects

But apart from the purely practical ways of coping with money worries there is also the emotional side to be considered. A lot of unhappiness about money comes about because people's expectations are not fulfilled. If you have studied hard for years in the hopes of getting a well-paid job and then can't get one you are bound to feel dissatisfied and let down. But it is vital not to let money worries get out of control, and to remember that the quality of life is more important.

If you wake up in a cold sweat night after night, wondering how on earth you are going to make ends meet, you are not only losing sleep, you are also wasting time. Tonight, when this happens, get up, get that sheet of paper out and do those sums and calculations.

Many people go through life being disorganised about money, and if you are one of them, just putting into practice a few basic plans on your budget will help. Once you get the system going it will run more or less on its own. Knowing your income and expenditure, having a file for every different bill, keeping your bank manager or building society manager in the picture will make you stronger, not only financially but emotionally too. You will feel better because you are in control and there will only be one further hurdle to surmount, that of letting money worries become a habit.

It is very easy to worry about money all the time, to let it take over so that, even though you are organised, you won't or can't allow your planning and management to be flexible. But provided you know where you are going with your money you can afford to start to enjoy it. Put aside the guilt and start to get some pleasure from that hard-earned cash. Make sure you always have some treat in store, whether it's a meal out or a weekend away.

At the same time, don't allow yourself to be so hidebound that you let good opportunities pass you by. If you have that solid organised basis to your finances you can afford – both practically and emotionally – to seize the chance of taking the odd financial gamble. Don't turn down the chance of a weekend away just because it hasn't been carefully planned for. Go and enjoy yourself, and spread the cost out over the next few weeks.

Above all, next time you find yourself getting depressed about money, be firm and repeat to yourself that you, and not your money, are going to control your life.

8

Friends – Who Needs Them?

When life is going well you probably have quite a list of people you know. You chat to them on the phone, meet for lunch, a drink in the pub, or at parties, and when you are with them, sharing a joke or having a lively discussion, you feel really close. You may be sure that in a crisis they'll all stand by you.

But now that crisis has come and what has happened? It's highly likely that that healthy list of people has shrunk to just a few because there's nothing like another's misfortunes to make people run a mile, whether from embarrassment, boredom or sheer lack of concern.

The trouble is that very few of us are totally honest with our friends. Most of the time we put on something of an act, we hide our true feelings of doubt or unhappiness, even when these are transitory. We make a big effort to be interesting company all the time, terrified that if we are not no one will want to know us.

The result is a series of friendships without depth – many things are hidden and not discussed.

Obviously you have to keep a sense of proportion. People who insist on baring their souls all the time are no more successful at keeping friends than those who draw a veil over their inner feelings. But if you have always kept yourself to yourself you are going to find it hard to reveal your pain. What you desperately need right now is someone who understands, someone who loves you enough – as a friend, not necessarily as a lover – to spare the time and patience to listen to you. In other words, a real friend.

Finding Real Friends

Not many of us have such friends; someone we've not only known for some time, but to whom we have become very close. You cannot have room in your life for more than a handful of really close friends because such friendships make demands, both in time and emotion. Like good marriages, friendships are not made overnight. They

57

need to be worked on, cultivated, fed and that takes time. That's why a best friend is often a husband, wife or lover, although it can just as well be an old school or college friend, or it could be someone you've not known very long but with whom you 'clicked' right from the start. Whichever way, the person whose company you crave is someone who understands you, someone with whom you have been completely honest up till now, someone who really knows you. If there is no one you can treat in this way, you may have to steel yourself to expose a side of your character that you have carefully hidden. Often you may only need to make a very small move; a simple phrase such as 'I'm really desperately unhappy' could be enough to bring the barriers down.

Everyone reacts differently to another person's pain, and only by trial and error will you be able to discover how friends are going to react to your tears, anger or bitterness. Unless you have just got one person to lean on, you are likely to turn to several people for comfort, advice, support, and everyone will have something different to offer. Make the most of the positive qualities of each person in your life.

A lively, consistently cheerful friend may find it terribly embarrassing when you break down in floods of tears, but you can use him or her as a way of getting out and about occasionally so that you can push that pain into the background for a while. A quiet, more introverted friend probably won't be able to cope with any high drama from you, but will always be happy to spend a peaceful evening talking and you can gain comfort from that.

Someone who has been through a crisis similar to your own could be a great help, but remember that his way of reacting to a crisis may not be yours. Someone who has recently been divorced may be relieved while you feel that your world has ended. Also, people who have not really worked through their pain often have extremely short memories – a year or even six months after the crisis, they cannot remember how they felt, what the depression was really like. They can talk for the present and tell you you'll soon feel better, but that won't be too comforting. So unless you feel they can be of real help, use these people for practical rather than emotional comfort.

The Friends You Don't Need

There are some friends you would do well not to rely on too much at the moment.

There are the impatient ones – probably acquaintances rather than friends, people with whom you have always put on a good show of being the life and soul of the party. Turn to them for comfort and they may listen for a while but in the end they'll lose patience. They will either drop you socially or tell you to pull yourself together. They may force wild parties on you when you are at your most vulnerable. These people believe in miracles and think that a word from them will put everything right. When it doesn't they become discouraged. And the worst of it is that *their* failure to comfort you makes *you* feel guilty for not trying hard enough.

Be wary about confiding in anyone who can make you feel inadequate. You know the type. They've suffered in the past but have pulled out of it very quickly. Their lives are highly organised and efficient, and if they have problems they are only transitory ones. They can't understand why others can't cope with life as efficiently as they do. They'll offer competent suggestions as to how you can cheer yourself up and be absolutely amazed when they don't work. People like this can only undermine your shaky feeling of confidence – if you let them in on your life now they'll only make you feel more down than you were before.

This applies especially if you are depressed about being overweight. Avoid those ex-fatties who had more willpower than you and are now slim and lithe, unless they're really sympathetic.

Steer clear of friends who have been depressed and haven't worked through broken relationships, bitterness, and so on.

Finally, beware of the hypercritical friends. You enjoyed their company before everything began to go wrong. *Then* you admired their lively minds, their bright ideas, the way they always managed to drive straight to the heart of a problem. *Now* they are still full of ideas but mostly concerned with what you shouldn't be doing, never anything really constructive about what could be done to help.

Making the Most of the Friends You Have

In the same way as you use those around you, like your family, to help you find comfort, so you can now use your friends. If you have always enjoyed going out to theatres and concerts with friends don't stop now because you are without a partner or because you feel too miserable to go. Those friends may hesitate to invite you, but try to make it clear you are still interested, and if they do make the first move think very carefully before you refuse.

The trouble with our society is that once people marry or begin to live together they tend to do everything as a couple. Even if one partner had plenty of separate interests beforehand, these tend to get dropped. This is a mistake, as you may well be discovering right now, for if one half of the partnership goes, the other is left high and dry.

If you were recently half of a couple and are now alone you may find an unwelcome change in your social life. The worst offenders are women towards other women. It is surprising how close and united other couples can suddenly become when the female sees a lone woman on the horizon. So many widows or divorcees suddenly find themselves relegated to coffee morning friendships whereas they and their partners were welcome dinner guests. If you are in this situation and you *are* invited to a dinner party it is highly likely that a suitable (or rather unsuitable) 'partner' for the evening will be laid on to even up the numbers and it is usually only in fiction that such pairing leads to happiness ever after.

If you have acquaintances who are so narrow-minded, give them a wide berth, or at least just use them when it suits you. After all, an occasional evening out may help, and if you return home feeling upset at the sight of all that matrimonial harmony it will do no harm at all to indulge in a few bitchy feelings and remind yourself that few couples are as blissfully happy as they like to pretend.

If you are lucky enough to have friends who are open-minded as well as open-hearted, your social life will not suffer too much. It is the people who have always regarded you as a person in your own right rather than as one of a pair who will still value you now that you are alone.

If you are depressed for other reasons than that of losing a love, it is worth accepting invitations out to dinners, small parties, concerts, cinemas, or whatever. If you really don't feel up to coping then say so, but don't cut off all channels of help of this kind. Tomorrow or in a few days time you will feel a little stronger, so never say 'no' outright to an invitation and, however bad you may feel, try to accept one occasionally. People have only so much patience and if you keep rejecting their offers they may well give up trying.

Some of your friends may want to help without knowing how to go about it. Try booking extra theatre seats and inviting friends to join you, and remember that you can also return those dinner invitations – giving a dinner party of your own will restore your confidence and also give you the chance to prepare a decent meal.

Friends who don't live just round the corner can also be useful. Plan ahead to go and visit them and maybe stay for a few days as a break. If you have recently been left alone it is very tempting to rush away at once – indeed some people suggest this, especially if you have been bereaved. The trouble is that sooner or later you are going to have to face up to going home, and dragging this out over several weeks or months is not going to help. You will begin to dread the inevitable moment and it will not help you to get through your early stages of grief. If there is a friend around who can help, you could organise for him or her to come and stay with you for a while, then try a period alone and then go away for a few days.

Visiting friends who have not shared every moment of your sadness or gloom is refreshing. You can talk about your worries and problems without feeling you are imposing on their hospitality, and the change of surroundings will doubtless do you good too. Because you have had little time to think things through you could well find the help and support they offer you seem more useful than that coming from friends who have been with you all along. Getting away from your immediate surroundings can help you to see things in a better perspective, too.

Keeping in Touch

If you have a telephone your bills are going to rocket right now – but if it's instant communication you are after, the telephone, if used properly, can be a great source of comfort. It is perfect for those quick, desperate calls to close friends when all you need to say is, 'Come over, I need to talk', or for a friend, who knows you are down, to call and invite you over for the day, morning or evening.

And when you are alone the sound of the telephone ringing can make you feel better almost at once. It is an immediate and positive sign that someone, somewhere . . .

So do encourage your friends to telephone you and don't hesitate to phone them.

Using the telephone

Although the telephone is such an important part of our lives most of us don't really know how to use it to its best advantage, and that's why a telephone conversation can sometimes make you feel worse rather than better. So you need to learn to make the best use of the telephone as a comfort source.

Don't let your telephone become too impersonal. If you sense that this is happening – in other words, if you feel even more isolated and depressed when you put the phone back on the hook – start to use it more positively, just to arrange dates and meetings, and confine your chats with people to face-to-face encounters. If you sometimes feel very cut off, use the telephone to get in touch with support groups for the depressed like the Samaritans – someone there will always be happy to listen to you and there is never any feeling of pressure for you to get off the line.

Remember that misunderstandings can easily arise over the phone. If you can't see the caller's face or expression you can easily find yourself taking things the wrong way, especially if you feel hypersensitive at the moment. If you lose your temper and hang up in the middle of a call, try to phone back at once to sort things out.

The telephone can also be very frustrating. If you break down in tears in the middle of a call your friend at the other end can do little more than make soothing noises, especially if he or she is miles away. If it all gets too much and you have to hang up, do phone back, or answer the phone if it rings later on; otherwise your friends will think the worst.

Tell yourself, too, that although you do pay for every second of a phone call, at a time like this money must take second place. The top priority is the contact you are having with the person who is giving you comfort, so if you are using the phone to talk about your problems, try to forget that it is there. Don't feel you have to talk non-stop – just as you would allow silences in normal conversation, do the same on the phone. A few moments of silence while you gather your thoughts or while your friend thinks of the best thing to say are just as valuable as the saving of a few extra pennies in phone costs.

Writing letters

A cheaper and just as comforting way to keep in touch is by letter. If you have a friend living some way away, write instead of phoning long distance. A letter will allow you to put your feelings down more clearly, and in doing this, you will be able to make some sense of what you are going through.

If it is advice and comfort you are after, you will probably get more back in letter form than in the spoken word. And it has the added advantage of being permanent. If you get a really comforting letter from a friend, full of good thoughts, pin it up somewhere where you can see it. Underline any important sections and glance at them every so often.

A letter written by you also means a reply and, as most post these days seems to consist of bills and circulars, a few personal letters are very welcome.

You may find it helpful to make copies of the letters you write, not only to stop yourself repeating things, but also to remind yourself in the weeks to come of how you felt. Charting the course of your recovery and the improvement, however slight, that each week brings is very comforting, and also helps you to see where you may be going wrong. Another way to record your progress is to keep a diary but many people find this hard to do even though they may not hesitate to write similar words to a friend.

Dropping in on friends

Whether you like or loathe the idea of people dropping in unannounced depends on your lifestyle. On the negative side, if you are feeling and looking your most miserable an out-of-the-blue knock at the door can be the final straw. On the positive side, for a friend to catch you at your worst may prove a blessing in disguise, especially if you have done a good cover-up job on how you really feel. A chance like this could allow you to admit your true feelings.

And an unexpected visitor on a day you thought had nothing in store is a comfort in itself.

Though you can't organise this sort of comfort, you can make it clear to your friends that they are welcome to drop in when they feel like it.

Turning the tables and dropping in unannounced yourself is another solution. Remember that you are the one who needs the attention now, so time your 'casual' visits fairly carefully so that you don't clash with your friends' commitments.

Are You Lonely or Just Alone?

There is a vast difference between being alone and loneliness. The former is something you can do out of choice and you can positively enjoy the peace and tranquillity that comes from having time to yourself, privacy that no one else need intrude on. Too many people lack this in their lives, or are afraid of what it might mean, and as a result become strained, tense and depressed.

Loneliness is different. You can live the high life, go to parties every night, lunch out with friends every day and still be devastatingly, deeply lonely.

Loneliness is a feeling of isolation, of not belonging, of always feeling out of touch. It can be having friends but not being able to be close to them. Or it can mean not having any friends because you are unable to create the perfect sort of close friendship you desire.

Maybe your sadness now comes from this feeling of loneliness. You want to have people around you but so far you have failed to find the right people. The trouble with friendship is that it can't be relied on to come up out of the blue, though this does sometimes happen. Mostly, though, it takes time to make friends and you probably feel at the moment that time is something you don't have.

You want help now, not tomorrow. You want comfort now, not in a few hours' time. You want friends now, not next week.

If there is no one in your life at the moment to whom you feel you can turn, no one who immediately comes to mind as a close friend, a best friend, or even a potential friend, or if the person you considered your best friend has left or died, then it is easy to feel depressed, lonely, deprived and even jealous of others who seem to have any number of friends to call on.

But you don't need to despair. Take comfort from this thought – you can be your own best friend. If you have taken time to think about yourself, about who and what you are, then no one else can know you as well as you now know yourself – your strengths and your weaknesses.

Outside friendships need nurturing; you have to give a lot in order to receive a lot in return. So, if you have never done so before, why not think about giving more of that time and attention and caring to yourself.

Most of us willingly sit down and spend hours listening to our friends' problems and we expect them to do the same for us. But if the right friends aren't around or the people you know aren't saying the right words, why not devote a little care and love to yourself. All those comforting words are there for you to use.

It will also give you a chance to re-value yourself – upwards. As you come to have a greater regard for yourself, you will relax more about outside friendships, and so make them more easily because you will be going out to find them from a position of strength. Realising that you can manage well without close friends will tend to make you a more attractive person, and it really does seem much easier to meet people and form friendships when you are not walking round with an air of desperation.

Making New Friends

Being virtually friendless happens to all sorts of personalities. Extrovert types normally have plenty of acquaintances but can have just as many problems making close friends as an introvert – they just take different forms.

If you are an extrovert you are probably surrounded by people who enjoy your company. For years you have hidden any sad feelings but now your hurt is too strong to bear. Habit may still stop you from revealing it but secretly you would love to stop acting the clown and allow your friends to give you the comfort you need. And you can do just that. As an extrovert half your work is done, all you have to do is mould the people around you to your new mood. Only you can judge which of your numerous friends can provide your various comfort needs – and in your search, try not to overlook the advantages of having some calmer, quieter people round you too.

If you are an introvert or a loner by nature, the loss of a love or any sort of depression will drive home to you very forcibly the drawbacks of keeping yourself to yourself. Of course now it will be much harder to go out and make contact with other people, but one of the best ways to overcome your hesitancy is to keep reminding yourself that you are a worthwhile person, that the time you have spent alone has given you more time to get to know yourself and that as a result you have a more complete personality to present to the rest of the world.

In the end we all have to find our salvation alone, but it does help to have someone around even if you just use them as a bouncing board for ideas. You may disagree with every single piece of advice they give you, but instead of allowing this to make you annoyed regard it positively as a way of allowing you to see what you want and need more clearly.

If you have ever tried to offer comfort and advice to someone who is confused, bitter, angry or depressed you'll remember how difficult it is. Unhappy people tend to be very perverse – you can present them with an indisputable truth and they'll deny it. Remember this when you are the one being comforted.

The usual advice to people looking for friends is to join a class or a group of some kind. This has been used so often that people tend to ignore it but it does get you away from home, it will occupy your mind and maybe even stimulate you to change your job or way of life. What it won't necessarily do is find you friends.

You can raise the odds on making friends by changing your approach slightly.

Conventionally we make friends gradually. If we are hesitant about baring our souls to people we have known for years then we are even more circumspect about doing so with casual acquaintances. But this way lies role-playing and the trap of putting on a personality that will appeal to society – being what we think we should be rather than what we are.

So the first rule is to be yourself. There's no need to go to extremes but, unless it really makes you feel a lot better, there is little point in pretending to be cheerful when you feel like crying and there is no

FRIENDS – WHO NEEDS THEM?

harm at all in being honest and telling even new friends that your lover has just walked out on you or you've lost your job.

The advantage of this approach is that it cuts out the social waffle and gives everyone a chance to be honest and open, leading in turn to a greater likelihood of making real friends.

Group therapy

One area where people do manage to break down the social barriers is in various forms of group therapy. If you are not used to expressing your emotions this could be the answer but be careful what you choose and where you go.

Some forms of group therapy are emotionally very violent, and little or no follow-up is provided. You could emerge from an hour of screaming abuse to find yourself very much as before and maybe even feeling ashamed.

Any kind of relaxation therapy (see chapters 3 and 6) such as yoga, meditation and tai chi can be helpful if you are feeling tense. The people you meet there will be attending for similar reasons and you may find you all have a lot in common.

Clubs specifically for the lonely, divorced, widowed, separated or whatever may also be helpful. It is comforting to meet others in a similar position to yourself, and will make you feel far less isolated, but it needs to be mixed with some other activity in order to keep a balance.

To sum up, if you have friends now is the time to use them. Turn to them for help and comfort but remember that their patience won't be unlimited, and that if you keep ignoring their advice you will be well on the way to losing them.

If you have no friends now is the time to start making them. Each day remind yourself that you are a worthwhile person with a great deal to offer. We all fail to appreciate ourselves enough, and really we should all make it our mission in life to be for rather than against ourselves. Feeling like this will show in the way you look and behave, you'll become more approachable, and the likelihood of finding friends will be that much greater.

In the meantime don't let a day go by without making contact with someone, even if it's only the guard at the station or the lady in the newspaper shop. Show you care about others and hopefully it will encourage others to care about you.

9

Love, Sex and Relationships

Most of us see a loving relationship as one of the fundamental keys to happiness. A brilliant career, an outstandingly varied sex life, all kinds of material comforts – we would set all of them to one side in favour of the perfect relationship.

To love and be loved equally in return does indeed create a terrific sense of well-being and balance that easily spills over into other areas of your life. Many apparent symptoms of ill-health – headaches, tiredness, irritability – can be dispelled if you have a harmonious relationship with a loved one. And it can also give you the extra strength to survive quite major disasters in other areas of your life. But in order for love to grow and flourish it needs attention and constant care.

What sort of love are we talking about anyway? Most of the time what people imagine to be love is not really love at all. It is in fact an addiction, a clinging to some sort of security or a familiar person. This has its dangers as it creates a relationship in which neither partner can thrive or develop because of the chains which bind them tightly together.

Addictive love fears change most of all. It is not a joyous feeling because it is based partly on fear and partly on habit. A healthy love will allow either partner in the relationship a lot of freedom to do what they enjoy because if you really love someone you will be anxious for them to change if necessary and be prepared to give them the chances to do so.

Of course this is never easy and there will always be limits to how much one person can give without becoming a doormat or almost irrelevant in the relationship. Still, there are many couples around who do not even allow each other to have separate friends, even if they are of the same sex, who object when one partner wants to pursue a favourite hobby that will take him or her away from home or who, socially, never lose sight of each other. This type of insecurity and lack of trust often only affects one partner and the effect on the relationship in the long-term can be devastating, as the more secure partner builds up a reservoir of resentment and frustration over the years.

So, in a loving relationship, it is crucial to try to learn to relax, trust your partner and both maintain lives of your own as well as the one you enjoy sharing. It's not easy and often the reasons for such insecurity and clinging lie a long way away from the actual relationship and these will need to be unearthed and dealt with – either on your own, with your partner or with the help of a therapist. Feeling secure about yourself, building up your feelings of self-esteem, realising that you are a worthwhile person in your own right, will take much of the pressure off a relationship and give both you and your partner the sense of freedom that is so essential.

Losing a Partner

If your partner has just died or walked out of your life, you are probably suffering the most painful of feelings, those of being bereft, rejected or unloved.

If the relationship was a good one – and this will probably only apply if your partner has died – then, although you may have many regrets, the love aspect of your unhappiness will not be at the root of your sorrow. There are several organisations listed at the end of this book that exist to offer help and support to widows and widowers.

But if you have just been knocked sideways by the end of a marriage or affair or have just discovered that your partner has been unfaithful (and in recent surveys 50 per cent of husbands and around three out of ten wives have admitted to straying outside a marriage or relationship) then, as well as putting into practice all sorts of comfort plans, you can help yourself a great deal by spending time analysing why this has happened – and what you can do to prevent it happening to you again.

First of all, be honest with yourself. It is very easy, if you consider that you are the 'wronged' party, to put all the blame on your partner for leaving or being unfaithful. But, just as it takes two people to make a relationship, so it often takes two to break it. Maybe if you sit down now and try to think about things unemotionally you will recognise that the relationship was not as good as it might have been – that there were faults on both sides. In many ways, you may eventually feel relieved that it is all over, that one of you has had the courage to step away and make the break, although of course this does not apply in the case of infidelity or adultery when the break-up of your relationship may not even be considered as a possibility by the partner who has erred.

There's no doubt that discovering that your partner has been sleeping with someone else – whether it's been a one-night stand or a long-running affair – is a shattering experience. For many people the first reaction – and a natural one – is to end the relationship. Being advised to forgive and forget has a very hollow ring to it. Once your initial anger and bitterness has passed and you feel a little calmer you need to decide, first of all, if the relationship is worth saving. If you are married and have children it will not be an easy decision. Either sit down and talk frankly to your partner about what has happened and why, or go together to somewhere like the Marriage Guidance Council for impartial advice and support.

If you decide to keep the relationship going you are going to have to forgive the lapse, even though you may never forget it and inevitably, in any row, you'll find it almost impossible to avoid accusations of what happened. From then on *both* of you will have to work at getting the relationship back onto a firmer footing. In the end you may even benefit.

Sexually you may find it hard to be at all giving, but it can be the first sign that life can go on, that you have it in you to be generous spirited – so refusing to make love could exacerbate the situation.

If you yourself are the one who has been unfaithful and are torn apart with guilt you will have to decide whether the affair should be ended, brought into the open, or, if your partner doesn't suspect, whether you should simply say nothing about it. Too many people who have been unfaithful tell their unsuspecting partners and cause a lot of distress simply because they can't cope with their own feelings of guilt. But since infidelity is really a betrayal of trust it seems reasonable that the price for the unfaithful partner should be some sleepless nights and the discomfort of having to keep the knowledge to themselves.

What went wrong?

The important thing to remember is that no pain of loss or failure is ever totally negative. If your marriage or affair has failed then it is up to you to learn from what went wrong, to stand back and look at the relationship honestly from both sides and see the mistakes made by both of you.

Spend some time working out for yourself what you would like from a new relationship, and what you would like to be able to put into it. For instance, it could be that your partner just happened to be a bit of a loner, someone who didn't really want to give or receive a lot of attention, whereas you were longing to give a lot and found yourself being rejected. Or maybe it was the other way round and you were too self-absorbed and selfish to be able to give much of yourself.

As you think these things through you are giving yourself time to recover and, though it could take months or even years, time spent in self-analysis now will be worth it in the long run.

Try to ignore the withdrawal symptoms or at least don't be too easily misled by them into another relationship too early on. If you have just emerged from an addictive relationship you will be longing for your daily 'fix' and the temptation to settle quickly for another relationship, any relationship, will be very strong.

One of the hardest things to accept at the end of a relationship is the knowledge that no one is indispensable. Most people take this as the final insult, but this is wrong. A relationship run on this basis won't be very happy or whole. Binding someone to you either by doing everything for them so they become totally dependent or by piling responsibilities on them that they morally can't push aside is not evidence of love, it is a form of trap – and not a tender one either.

What you may now find offered to you is a chance, maybe the best chance you have ever had, to find and prove that you can stand alone. Just as you may have come to enjoy your own company when friends were in short supply, so you need to feel a similar feeling towards love relationships. You need to develop a respect for yourself as a complete person, not just as one half of a partnership. Once you have learnt to live happily alone, you will be truly ready to go into a new relationship. To this relationship you will be able to bring your whole self.

Improving a Relationship

But maybe life isn't so cut and dried. Agonising as it may be to have to face up to the loss of someone you have loved, it is often worse to be in an existing relationship and to be aware that it is going wrong or is not as good as it might or could be. Living with someone on this basis is very depressing. If you haven't been able to pin down the cause of your depression, even though you have gone through all the other possible reasons, now may be a good time to take a hard look at your marriage or affair and see how healthy it is.

Ask yourself the following questions, and answer them honestly:

1 Presumably you had your own friends and interests before you met – have you retained any of them?
2 Have you developed new interests and made new friends of your own since the relationship began?
3 When your partner has to go away do you dislike being apart?
4 If your partner wanted to go away alone for a while would you agree willingly and lovingly?
5 If everything went wrong between you can you imagine remaining friends afterwards?

If you have answered 'no' to any one of the above five questions then your relationship is not as good as it could be. Maybe the lack of freedom your partner imposes is getting you down, maybe you only do things together and you secretly find this frustrating, but whatever the reasons there is no need to despair.

The answer is not necessarily to end the relationship, or even to have a trial separation – far too many people walk out of relationships and back into them a few months later, and change nothing.

The more long-standing the relationship the more difficult it will be to change. Over the years reactions will have become almost stereotyped, and bad old habits are the most difficult to change.

Your first step is to talk to your partner but if you find it difficult to work things out between you, there is no harm in calling in outside help like that of a marriage guidance counsellor – they exist to improve existing relationships as well as counsel broken ones.

But to get you started, as well as sitting down and discussing things with your partner, try the following.

Take the occasional break from each other. It could just be an evening or day out alone, or maybe a couple of days away on a course.

If your relationship is very introverted, make a point, over the next few weeks, of going out together but spending the time mixing with others separately.

Try to establish a precedent that there are some areas of your life that are yours alone – and the same for your partner. At the same time, if they don't already exist, create areas of common interest.

Best of all, sit down with your partner and devise some rules just for the two of you that you both feel will improve and strengthen your relationship.

Relationships after Divorce

If your marriage or relationship breaks up and there are no children your reactions towards each other can be as frank, angry or even friendly, as you like. If you decide never to see each other again and that you will hate each other for the rest of your lives that is entirely up to you – but if there are children from the relationship all this changes.

You can no longer just think of yourself. You have to think of your children and the effect this break-up is having on them. There is no way that divorce or separation can be made completely painless for a child. Even parents who have gone to great lengths to keep things friendly may find, years later, that their children harboured fantasies of their parents getting together again and even found their friendship slightly bewildering.

However, this sort of bewilderment can be dealt with and will probably not cause any real damage. The children who do suffer the most are those who find themselves in the middle of their parents' anger and who often feel that they are to blame.

So it is part of your parental responsibility to ensure that your children suffer as little as possible. This has a big advantage – by behaving as well as you can under the circumstances, by putting your children's needs before your own feelings, you may actually end up feeling better. Think of it this way. If you direct your anger with your partner through your children – for instance by telling them that their father or mother is worthless, a bastard because he/she has left, by refusing access or by making access disagreeable, you are creating even more bad feelings – and what is worse you are insisting that your children share in them.

Of course it is not easy, if you've effectively been left holding the baby, to be calm and fairly amenable, but it is certainly worth trying. If you find that the anger and bitterness are so overpowering that you cannot control them when you talk then a sensible answer is to try and organise communication with your partner through a third party. Don't spend hours haranguing each other over the phone or, unforgiveably, in front of the children. Whatever your feelings about your partner your children have the right to his/her love and time – and to be able in time to make their own judgements.

Access is often a fraught area. As the partner who has left you must be absolutely reliable and stick to arrangements. As the one who has the children you must do likewise, and if you cannot bear to see your partner then arrange to take the children to a mutual friend on access days from where they can be collected. If you find you cannot agree on access then seek advice from an objective third party. Some solicitors are helpful, and if you are already involved in court proceedings you may be able to be referred to the court welfare officer for help. The other option is to go to one of several conciliation groups up and down the country – your local Citizens Advice Bureau will be able to tell you if there is one in your area or at least something that provides an equivalent service.

Money is another area that is fraught with problems and often couples who have managed their separation or divorce quite calmly will find that finances is the one area of contention.

It's worth remembering that divorce in particular rarely benefits either partner financially – running two homes instead of one is bound to be more expensive. But you cannot separate money from emotions in these circumstances so try, if you can, to get the best deal possible without falling into the trap of insisting on more just to be vindictive (or paying less than you can honestly afford for the same reason).

Divorce and remarriage
Oddly enough the most traumatic time after divorce can come when

a partner remarries – even if this occurs years later when you have worked through your initial feelings of loss.

Many men and women who appear to have come to terms with divorce suddenly go to pieces when their partner remarries – although it is true to say that women suffer most here, even if they themselves have remarried.

Suddenly all the anger, bitterness and grief resurface, and it comes as a terrible shock to realise that you can still feel so strongly. Often it makes little difference whether you ended the relationship or not, or even whether you get on with the new wife or husband. Of course the pain is exacerbated if the new partner is younger, or seemingly more talented or more attractive.

What you are experiencing is the final death of the relationship and probably for the last time all the old doubts will be raised – could we have made it work, what has he/she got that I haven't? And this tends to happen only on remarriage – the other partner living with someone else is somehow more acceptable or bearable.

Remember that what you feel is normal – don't try to suppress it. Talk about it to a good friend or a counsellor or therapist. It rarely lasts as long as the earlier pains of divorce and is a vital stage you need to pass through before beginning life afresh – or continuing the lifestyle you have established.

Your Sex Life

At its best sexual intercourse can make you feel the most loved and loving, the most cared for and caring person in the world. It is not just the physical pleasure it gives that is so important but also the marvellous sensation of being so close, so united with someone that you are both giving and receiving pleasure in equal amounts. The touching involved in sexual encounters is also a vital part of the whole and something that is easily overlooked or undervalued.

There are two ways in which your sex life could be depressing you now. Either you have been used to a regular sex life and this has now finished or, although you have a partner, sex between you is becoming a disaster area with either or both of you off the whole idea.

Life Without Sex

If you have had a good sex life until recently you are going to miss it badly. It is not just the orgasms you achieved but you are also deprived of that feeling of being wanted, held, touched – and your own desire to touch and give is, for the time being, thwarted.

If your partner has rejected your body and bed in favour of someone else's then the blow to your ego is tremendous. When people make love they usually give far more than just their bodies, and they end up revealing far more than their physical appearance, so rejection on this level is terribly painful. How you react will depend not only on your personality and age but also on your libido – in other words how important sex is to you.

Sex for Comfort

A few years ago it would have been quite acceptable, if you needed sex, to sleep with the first available partner – although you would have still had to think carefully about it beforehand, mainly to ensure that by indulging in casual sex as a source of comfort, you were not going to increase your feelings of inadequacy. But times have changed. Although moral considerations may well stop you from frequent sexual encounters, far more worrying are the risks you run if you do so.

AIDS (Acquired Immune Deficiency Syndrome) is now killing hundreds of people a year in this country. If you are homosexual, bisexual, a drug addict or haemophiliac you are in the high risk category. Ordinary heterosexuals are not at such great a risk but the chances of catching AIDS obviously increase if you start going to bed with people you barely know or frequently changing sexual partners. It is not just AIDS which can cause you to worry – the incidence of other sexually transmitted diseases is also rising and many of them are becoming increasingly resistant to treatment.

With all this in mind sexual intercourse for the sake of comfort becomes a very dubious, not to say life-threatening, exercise. And even entering into a new relationship on a serious basis is something you must do with care and thought.

There are some ways round this. For a start, if you are looking for comfort this need not be found in full intercourse – simply touching, fondling, mutual masturbation – but not oral or anal sex – are excellent alternatives and with the right person can bring you a great deal of joy.

However if full intercourse is on the cards you *must* be prepared. Obviously for a woman contraception is vital but these days both men and women should always carry a supply of condoms – and use them. As a woman the idea of carrying around your own supply of condoms may shock you – you may fear that you'll be thought of as somewhat fast. But if it's a question of being misjudged on that basis or catching a life-threatening disease, it's clear where your priorities should lie.

Celibacy

Opting to be celibate – not to have a sex life – is a positive step to take if you are feeling vulnerable. It is a choice you can make for yourself and although you may feel frustrated at first this soon wears off and your sexual desire will decrease. Celibacy has enjoyed quite a fashion in the States in recent years and of course it is not something you have to keep to for life!

Where to Find a Partner

Whether it's a sexual relationship you want or just a very close friendship, finding someone to share your life is never easy. All the places mentioned in the chapter on friends are equally good for long-term relationships but there are other alternatives.

Advertising

Many people would baulk at the very idea of advertising for friendship. It seems such an admission of failure, so blatant. But if you think about it you stand as good a chance of meeting someone compatible through an ad as you do if you go to a party – ten to one in both cases you will be meeting a total stranger and why not one who already knows a little about you?

In many ways you will be better off if you place your own ad rather than answering one. Try not to embroider the truth – there's no point in describing yourself as 5 foot 8 inches, slender and beautiful if you are in reality 5 foot 2 inches and the only person who thought you beautiful was your mother! If looks are not your strong point then highlight some other aspect – a sense of humour, the fact that you are a brilliant pianist or whatever. By placing your own ad you not only get to choose the wording and description, you can also filter the replies, talk, write, exchange photographs with possibles before you even meet.

As in life there will be disappointments, but provided you are clear in your own mind what you want from this new relationship then you may be one of the lucky ones and find a soulmate. Even if you don't, but approach the exercise in the right frame of mind – regarding it as a chance to get out and about, talk and exchange ideas, then you have little to lose.

Computer Dating

Here again you must be honest when giving information – and hope that others are doing likewise. People have been known to live happily ever after thanks to this form of encounter but a computer is only a machine – it can match up various pieces of information but only as much as it is given and certainly without the little nuances that can make or break a relationship.

Marriage Bureaux

A reputable bureau should have staff trained to match up various personalities – and the advantage is that you receive a personal service. It costs more too, but if you are at all hesitant about meeting people, you may find it easier to use this form of dating. It still doesn't guarantee that you'll meet the love of your life!

Going It Alone

Maybe you need sexual relief but you have no-one to go to bed with, or feel morally and emotionally that you can only sleep with someone you love.

Touching yourself can only be good for you, and a lot of people find it easier to orgasm through masturbation.

An orgasm is a very good tension reliever, and if you are alone you can work out for yourself exactly how you are going to masturbate.

Some people find simply touching themselves enough, others need the extra stimulation of a vibrator, an erotic picture, or even music.

Masturbation has several advantages. If you are completely alone it provides your body with the physical release it needs. If your sex life has never been very successful, masturbating can help you to learn a lot about how your body reacts, and in your next relationship you will be able to use this information to give and receive more pleasure. Finally, if you are so tensed up that your regular sex life is affected then masturbation can help to ease you back into feeling good again.

If You Are Off Sex

Even if your feelings of depression are not caused by the loss of a partner they can still affect your sex life.

Being unhappy in your marriage, being bored at work, losing a job, recovering from flu or any other illness, can all adversely affect your desire for sex – in short, you may go right off it. Depending on your attitude, your partner's attitude and your general awareness of what's happening, this state could last a matter of weeks or go on for months or even years.

The longer you and your partner go without making love the harder it may be in the end to get close together again. As you lie there refusing to make love you might spare the occasional thought for how your partner feels as his or her advances are rejected time after time.

On the other hand, to allow someone to have intercourse with you when you are not really willing or interested is as insulting as refusing outright to make love, and sex entered into in this unloving, uncaring way can be very damaging to both partners.

What to do

Obviously the first step is to recognise what is happening. For a man the signs are fairly obvious – impotence, premature ejaculation, failure to climax. As a woman you just never get worked up, no amount of stimulation will help you to orgasm or even enjoy what's going on.

Try to pinpoint why you feel like this, and talk about your feelings

80

with your partner. If the reasons are unconnected with your relationship this should be fairly easy; if, however, it is all due to the relationship being wrong or your partner being less than caring in bed, you still need to talk things over, but more tactfully.

On a practical level, you can help yourself and find comfort while waiting for your sexual feelings to reassert themselves.

Most important of all is to remember that there is more to sex than just the act of intercourse. Most relationships start out well – couples touch, feel, stimulate each other before they actually make love but as the years pass these acts of love gradually vanish and all that is left is sexual intercourse. So it's hardly surprising that if anything is wrong with life it shows itself in reactions between the sheets.

Doctors and therapists advise couples whose sex lives are going badly to abstain from sexual intercourse for a while. So try now to go back to the early days of your relationship, to the days when just to touch each other's bodies was a joy. What you need from your partner is the comfort that comes from being held and caressed. The pleasure that can come from someone gently touching you all over. The peace that results from someone holding you close as you fall asleep. And it doesn't have to be totally one-sided. You may find that if your partner caresses you gently for a while, you will want to reciprocate.

If you want to be more organised you can try massaging each other. You need oil for this – coconut or safflower, or any perfumed body oil, are ideal.

The floor is the best place for massage. Lie on a soft rug covered with a large towel or a couple of folded blankets. The room needs to be warm and dimly lit, and you need a bowl of hot water in which to stand another bowl of massage oil to warm.

As you are the one in need of comfort the idea is for your partner to massage you. Don't worry about techniques, all he or she will be doing is rubbing gently all over your naked body. If you like, you can have music in the background – and of course you must make sure you are not disturbed.

If you are depressed about yourself and your life a full body massage by the person you love, and who loves you, is an almost perfect form of comfort. By touching you all over, that person is affirming that you are cared for, that you matter.

The relaxation that comes from this sort of massage may well make you feel that sex is not such a bad idea after all, but don't worry if you simply feel like going to sleep.

Where Do You Go From Here?

Sorting out problems in an existing relationship or with your sex life takes time and a certain amount of dedication from both partners. Even if, in the end, you decide that there is really no future in the relationship and it is better to part you can go in the knowledge that you tried your best to make it work. Hopefully, in time, you will also be able to look back and see the good parts of the time you spent together.

One of the worst aspects of ending a relationship is that the final scenes are frequently those of anger or pain and overshadow what went before. Some people *do* get married knowing full well that they are making a mistake but have reached a point where they are too afraid or embarrassed to back out. But the majority do enter marriage full of the best intentions and convictions and maybe have several years of happiness before things begin to go wrong. It is these early years that need remembering from time to time – not in a maudlin way but as a reassurance to yourself that there was a time when you loved and were loved – and that time can come again.

If you have been badly hurt or feel a lot of bitterness and mistrust about the end of a relationship, the big hurdle is how you handle future involvements. Some people cope by dissociating themselves from any further commitments – their trust has been so badly undermined that they feel everyone will be the same, that they will always be ill-treated or betrayed.

Others, having been hurt by a member of one sex, may seek a solution by turning against that sex altogether. If, as a heterosexual, you can find comfort in a relationship with a member of your own sex that is sexual as well as emotional you must be careful that you are entering into this for the right reasons. Turning to a homosexual or lesbian relationship will not necessarily solve your deepest problems. Sooner or later in any relationship you will be faced with the choice you may be dreading – that of commitment.

It may sound easier to spend the rest of your life skirting round the edge of love. You can convince yourself that that way you will never be hurt or trapped again. Certainly if you have been through a very bad time you will not be ready emotionally. In fact, as the high divorce rate in second marriages shows, it is often better to take time to stand back and not get too involved too soon.

But your greatest loss, if you choose to live your emotional life on the sidelines, is that you will never give yourself the chance to experience a full relationship. Of course there are risks, and there will be pain and tears – but by allowing yourself to be open to these feelings, you can also experience the positive benefits – the closeness, the sharing, the moments of happiness.

What you need now most of all is time to recover. You need that time to look at what went wrong and to learn from the mistakes made on both sides. You also need time to establish a life for yourself on your own, particularly if the relationship just ended goes back over many years.

Through this you will give yourself a firm grounding and gain in confidence. You will begin to have a much better opinion of yourself as an individual rather than just as the other half of a partnership. Once you have achieved this – and it can often take quite a time – you will be ready, when the chance of a deep committed relationship comes along, to enter into it happily and not hesitate to give it all you can without being afraid.

10
And so to bed . . .

Well, you made it through another day. It may have been painful or upsetting or you may have coped pretty well. Now, the night has come round again, and whatever sort of day you have had, this still poses a challenge just as great as getting through a day and making the most of it.

What is it about the night that makes it such a daunting prospect if you are feeling down? For a start, however depressed you may feel as day breaks, at least there is always some hope, however faint, that this day will be an improvement on yesterday. At night-time everything is much more limited. If you have had a rotten day and pressures have built up, then the peace of the night is the perfect time for all your troubles and worries to come crowding in on you.

If you live anywhere but in a large city it is likely that by ten-thirty or eleven o'clock all life outside your home will have ceased – cinemas close, so do pubs, restaurants, cafés, corner shops. This general 'shutting down' at night isn't going to make you feel any better, and if you live on a busy main road this may be the one time in your life that you bless the roar of ten-ton trucks past your window.

The trouble is that night is such a private time. The darkness makes it clear that people have retreated into their own worlds and this heightens any feelings of loneliness, fear or despair. And of course the most difficult moment of all is going to bed and getting to sleep.

Do You Need Sleep?

We are all brought up to consider sleep as a most essential part of living. Children are told that without sleep they won't grow properly, they won't be able to work at school and so on. Adults, it seems, only have to mention to a doctor that they can't sleep and the prescription pad is filled with suitable pills to alleviate this terrible affliction.

Of course, the body does need sleep because it is only when you

84

are asleep that the system has time to rest. The heartbeat slows, the various organs tick over, gently digesting, cleansing, building. At the same time the brain, which has been on the alert all day long, also shuts down for the night, maintaining just enough activity to keep the body working. But while the major organs are at rest it gives other parts of the body system a chance to do a little overtime; many new cells, for instance, are made while we are asleep.

So some sleep is needed to keep the body physically healthy.

The emotions need sleep too. It is the one time when you can switch off mentally from all the immediate problems that occupy your mind during the waking hours. Admittedly, if you are very disturbed emotionally your thoughts will continue to haunt you in the form of dreams, but at least dreams often do not resemble reality too closely. And there is no doubt that a good night's sleep from which you awaken refreshed and calm does help you to cope with whatever the day may bring, whereas lack of sleep leaves you feeling tired and irritable, with nerves jangling, before the day's problems have even begun.

So does all this mean sleep at all costs, even that of risking becoming reliant on pills to achieve it?

First of all, unless you really are incapable of sleeping, and have genuinely not slept for several nights and are feeling the after-effects badly, do try some of the comfort remedies in this chapter or *talk* to your doctor about your problems before falling back on any sort of chemical drug to induce sleep. And if nothing else seems to work and you are given sleeping pills then do yourself a favour and use them sensibly. Try to do without them fairly soon, or only use them once in a while to give yourself a night of sleep.

But there are several forms of comfort you can experiment with at night before turning to pills for help.

First of all, look at your attitude towards sleep. Two things tend to happen when you've had several bad nights. First, you start to dread the approach of bedtime because you know you aren't going to sleep. Secondly, it is very easy to become obsessed by the absolute necessity for unbroken sleep. The body needs the rest induced by sleep, it is true, but the important word is rest rather than sleep.

Finally, it's worth bearing in mind that your mind often plays tricks on you. You may have slept in the same bed as someone who complains in the morning that he didn't sleep a wink, despite the fact that you saw him asleep. You have done it yourself. It is easy, if you wake a few times and take ages to drop off again, to assume that you didn't sleep at all. So, unless you have actually spent all night long out of bed or sitting up reading, give yourself the benefit of the doubt and assume you've snatched at least a couple of hours sleep in between waking; psychologically it will make you feel a little better.

Getting Ready for the Night

Late evening may be the one time you can guarantee you won't be interrupted, so make the most of this time as you prepare your body and your mind for a night's rest. For the moment don't think about sleep, concentrate on rest.

You can start quite early in the evening if you like, depending on what you've got planned. Don't, for instance, forgo an evening out with friends or at a concert, even if it's alone, just for the sake of preparing for bed. But if you have an empty evening ahead of you and you are already feeling tired – even if it's only 8.30 – there's no reason why you shouldn't start preparing for the night.

Remember that depression will often make you feel tired anyway. This may be due to boredom or it may just be your body trying to tell you that you've been through a hell of a lot of strain recently and need the rest.

Your surroundings

Just as it is important to make your bedroom an attractive place to be in if you are planning a whole *day* in bed, so it should be pleasant and soothing for night-time.

Is your bed as comfortable as it could be? Most people are pretty lackadaisical about beds, and buy the first that comes to hand without worrying about whether the mattress is too hard or too soft. As a result they have years of bad sleep without realising why, and only when other problems prevent their sleeping altogether does the discomfort of the bed become apparent. Obviously you can't just go out and spend a few hundred pounds on a new bed but you can adjust your old one to suit. If your mattress is too soft trying putting a board under it. If the bed is too hard and unyielding try a couple of blankets or an old eiderdown over the mattress.

What about your coverings – blankets or duvets? At the moment you may often feel cold in bed, probably because you're very tense, so you want to make sure you have enough coverings round to keep you warm. If you're already into duvets you'll know how comforting they can be, the way they sort of cuddle round you and enfold you. But if you swear by blankets and sheets, make sure you have extra blankets around to pile on in the dark before the dawn.

You may be a hot water bottle addict, and find cuddling one most comforting. If so, don't be ashamed to make yourself one even at the height of summer (it doesn't have to be filled with boiling hot water) because just to hold something warm against you in an otherwise empty bed is a great solace.

Electric blankets are also a great help. For a start, it is pleasant to clamber into a bed that is already warm and, best of all, when you wake up hours later chilled to the bone it's nice to be able to reach over and with a flick of the switch flood your bed with warmth.

You could also give those sheepskin rugs recommended for the elderly and frail a try. You put them under your bottom sheet and it makes the bed under your back feel very soft and warm. It doesn't matter if you are young and normally healthy – at the moment you are, in a sense, an invalid and deserve the extra comforts.

If you've spent most of your life going to bed naked maybe now is the time to put on your pyjamas or nightdress. This applies especially if you've lost your bed companion because you are going to feel much colder and even more abandoned without another person in the bed throwing out bodily heat or cuddling you. You need something close to the skin to comfort you, so choose nightwear in soft materials, such as fine wools, silks, or very soft cotton, but steer clear of nylon. Incidentally, the same applies to sheets and bed linen. Nylon sheets may be cheap and practical but they are not soothing, so make sure you have cotton, cotton/polyester or winceyette.

Now for the room around you. Like your bed, it needs to be warm and welcoming. As you walk into your bedroom at night it should make you feel that it's the best place in the world to be right now, that sleep and a peaceful night are almost inevitable.

Not many of us have bedrooms like that. They mostly seem to exist in the pages of magazines. Don't despair, because all you really need to do to hide the bright flowery wallpaper, the jazzy curtains and the threadbare carpet is to play a few tricks with the lighting.

If you don't feel in the mood for buying new lamps or shades, just replace most of your 100-watt bulbs with pink 60-watt ones. Light some candles too as you come to bed, but make sure they are in a safe place in case you just happen to drop off before blowing them out.

If you have an open gas or electric fire in the bedroom, light it. It will provide not only warmth but light too.

Buy some joss sticks, if you like them. They come in all sorts of perfumes and one long stick lasts for over fifteen minutes.

Try and organise some background music for your bedroom. You could use a portable cassette recorder – an all-in-one clock radio/cassette is ideal as you can choose your own taped music but still have the radio if you want it. If all your stereo equipment is downstairs you might consider having a lead run up to your bedroom and a small speaker installed.

If you are alone – or at least without a bed partner – you might consider not sleeping in your bedroom at all. Think about the number of times you've sat in the sitting-room feeling reasonably comfortable, warm and relaxed, maybe watching a late night film on television or listening to music or reading. And you have to break that mood to go upstairs to bed. If you're really exhausted you may have even dropped off in the course of the evening.

Well, you don't *have* to sleep in the bedroom, but you need to make sure that you're reasonably comfortable elsewhere. The advantage of a sitting-room is that it's likely to have better heating and so be warmer. And sleeping downstairs in a house means that you're closer to the kitchen and those middle-of-the-night drinks. You may have a large sofa to lie on; if so, bring in some covering so you don't get chilled. If there isn't anything to lie on and the idea of sleeping downstairs appeals to you, organise a mattress on the floor, a camp bed, a couple of eiderdowns or whatever, earlier on in the evening. Get your nightclothes ready too – sleeping in your day clothes isn't a good idea as you will wake feeling very rumpled and uncomfortable.

Before You Go To Bed

Wherever you are going to sleep, there are various reasons why you may want to start getting ready for bed as early as you can. If there are other people around they are just going to have to be understanding about your needs at the moment. If, for example, you find that by nine o'clock you are falling off your feet or can't bear to be in company for any longer, off you must go to bed.

On the other hand, you may be in such a state of fear about the long night ahead of you that you want to put off the evil moment for as long as possible. That's understandable but if you have got into a habit, not only of having bad nights but also of counteracting them by going to bed very late, it's worth trying to break this routine. Do this gently, not by going to bed earlier but by starting to prepare for bed earlier. That way you don't actually commit yourself to bed but you do give your body a chance to rest.

So what can you do to prepare yourself for bed, and hopefully sleep?

First of all, baths. Any of the baths mentioned in chapter 4 are suitable. What you want is a good long quiet warm soak – no interruptions, no pressure to get out of the bathroom. Allow at least half an hour.

A radio or a good book is a help but you may prefer to just lie and soak, topping up occasionally with warm water if possible. If you aren't reading, bathe by candlelight. When you get out of the bath cuddle the towel tightly round you and sit or lie for a while until you are nearly dry. Then, when you are dry, you can massage some oil into your body.

Night-time drinks

A warm drink is a good idea at some stage. You might like to take it into the bathroom to sip in there, or wait until you are actually in bed.

What to drink. You need something soporific, soothing and comforting. So go for a warm drink. Don't have tea or coffee as they will keep you awake. Here are some suggestions: Milk drinks are supposed to help you to relax so if you are the type who likes warm or hot milk – it makes some people feel sick – try mixing milk with any of the following: sugar, a couple of spoonfuls of honey, whisky, rum, cocoa, chocolate. Other alcoholic drinks, provided you don't have too much, also relax you. Try hot whisky and lemon or hot rum and lemon, mixing equal quantities of whisky and lemon juice, topping up with hot water, and adding sugar or honey to taste. Mulled wine is warming and comforting. Use any red wine, heat it gently in a saucepan with a teaspoon of cinnamon sprinkled on top and a couple of cloves, a lemon peel and sugar to taste.

Herbal teas are ideal nightcaps. Try camomile, peppermint mixed with a few dried sage and rosemary leaves.

Sleep exercises

If the night is the time you choose for exercise or yoga postures, you can do these either before or after your bath and you will find that they relax as well as exercise. Once you are in bed you can relax yourself further by going into a deep relaxation routine.

Lie on your back, hands by your sides, legs slightly apart and feet turned outwards. Clear your mind of all other thoughts except those about your body, and work your way up from your feet. Breathe slowly and deeply through your nose. Start with your feet; make them very tense, count to five and then relax. Do the same for legs, hands, arms, stomach, neck, shoulders, face.

At the end of this you should at least be very aware of the difference between relaxed parts of your body and tense parts. Now, with your eyes closed, let your mind drift onto something pleasant. If you can, evoke the same scenario each night until it becomes a habit. For instance, imagine you are floating in the sky surrounded by small white clouds. Your body feels weightless and you don't have to make any effort to move because a gentle breeze is taking care of that. All around is blue sky and puffy white clouds. The sun shines warm all over you. You can keep this image, or one of your own choosing, for as long as you like; for some lucky people it may actually induce sleep, for others it will hopefully just promote a feeling of relaxation.

If you feel very afraid and lonely at the moment there is no need to switch the light off to go to sleep. Leaving the light on has advantages – first, you avoid that moment of truth when you have to reach out and plunge the room into darkness, and secondly it is more comforting to wake in the night with some light around you.

The same applies to music. If you are enjoying your radio or tape but feel drowsy, don't bother to switch if off. Once again, by not switching off you will feel less lonely and if you do wake it will not be to that dreadful hollow silence of the middle of the night.

So far I've assumed that you are alone in bed but you are just as likely to feel depressed and still have to share your bed at night with your husband/wife or lover.

Theoretically at least, compared to those who are really alone, you do have the advantage of another human being beside you even if you are depressed. However, if the relationship is crumbling or going through a bad patch, you may wish desperately that you *were* alone.

First of all, if your relationship is fairly healthy and your depression is due to other reasons then make the most of that other person at bedtime. If your partner loves you and cares about you he or she will want to help.

Sex is a terrific relaxer but it has to be done in the right way. Making love just because you feel you ought to is not going to help you sleep – you won't enjoy it, neither will your partner, and you'll still lie there afterwards brooding.

If you can persuade your partner to be understanding, holding each other close is very comforting. So many couples only get really close when they are making love, then they roll their separate ways and go to sleep. What you need now is the comfort your mother gave you as a baby when she held you in her arms, and your partner can do that for you. Drifting off to sleep enfolded in someone's arms is about the most comforting way to cope with a sleep problem. And you can also try some of the massage techniques suggested in chapter 4, remembering that they don't have to be an inevitable prelude to lovemaking but can just be a way of making you feel wanted and cared for.

If your insomnia is really bad and relations are strained you may be tempted to sleep alone – but this could precipitate a 'thin end of the wedge' situation. If you yearn to be alone at night it may make better sense to take yourself off somewhere for a few days and nights, rather than establishing your aloneness at home.

On the other hand, if you can talk your feelings out with your partner, sleeping separately could work, because one of the worst problems with trying to get to sleep when there is someone else in bed with you is the extra tension it creates as you try desperately not to toss and turn too much.

Suppose You Really Can't Get To Sleep

You've tried everything, the bath, the drink, the relaxation. It's now several hours later and if anything you are more wide awake than ever. It's at this point that people get desperate; they squeeze their eyes tight shut, clench their fists and try and force themselves to sleep. It's really a waste of time – the thoughts drive through your mind and you feel like screaming. Lying in bed is doing no good at all, so you might as well get up or, if you are alone, sit up and do something constructive.

Research has shown that people can continue to function reasonably well on quite small amounts of sleep. You may be a type who has always needed eight hours a night but you can manage on less and you'll feel better if you don't try and force yourself into old routines which only worked when you were happy and relaxed.

If you can stay in bed, do. Have the light on, read, sew, get up briefly to make another drink if you like. Give yourself half an hour or so and then have another go at sleeping.

If you are not alone you are going to have to get up. If you do, try to keep warm. Wherever you choose to sit – kitchen or sitting-room – make sure you have a fire on or put on extra clothes.

When you get back to bed spend at least twenty minutes going through some relaxation routines. This is not a waste of time because it ensures that you are at least resting yourself so that if sleep evades you again you can comfort yourself with that thought.

In fact you should bear this in mind whenever you have a sleepless night. If you can spend some of the time consciously resting, you are doing yourself some good.

If You Wake in the Night

Insomnia takes many forms, not necessarily the obvious one of not being able to sleep at all. You may be so drained by the end of the day that you fall asleep very quickly, only to wake after three or four hours and be unable to fall asleep again.

This is tricky. Probably you have had just enough sleep to make you feel rested for the time being but not enough to make it easy to get through the next day with your eyes wide open and your mind clear.

Give yourself fifteen minutes or so to try and drop off to sleep again. In that time do the relaxation routines and try and keep your mind empty of worry.

If sleep still won't come, don't panic. Develop a positive attitude towards being awake at this time. You may feel hungry, in which case you are perfectly entitled to have something to eat. Make yourself another warm drink and if it won't disturb everyone have another bath.

While you are sitting down sipping your drink, if your sadness and worries are overwhelming, try writing down what you feel. Very often the emotions we have in the middle of the night are much more intense than those we have during the day. Uncluttered by the noise of other people and things the mind can sometimes see more clearly. Ideas that seemed confused earlier now become crystal clear. If that happens don't take the risk of forgetting all about these new insights or plans, get them down on paper.

You can do the same with all the things that worry you. Rather than lying in bed with your mind in turmoil, write a list of everything that is stopping you from relaxing and going to sleep. Seeing them in black and white may make you realise how insignificant some of them are and help you to get your priorities right for the next day.

Obviously you can't write these lists night after night so there's no harm in making night into day, as it were. After all, most of us barely find enough time during the day to do all we have to do in the home. So use being awake to get things done – ironing, mending a broken chair, knitting, sewing, cooking, reading, tidying shelves or drawers. Don't make it too strenuous or noisy, otherwise a few more problems will land on your plate. The main aim during this time of wakefulness is to think positive about being awake – you are not wasting your time tossing and turning in bed and your mind is probably more at ease than it would be if you had stayed in bed.

But try not to overdo it. You still have tomorrow to face. After about an hour go back to bed and have another go. With any luck you should manage to drop off to sleep again for a few more hours. If not, then stay where you are and read or, if that's going to disturb your bed companion, move to a comfortable room, put your feet up and read or listen to music there – but this time round, rest is the priority rather than activity.

If You Wake in the Early Morning

This is another common occurrence when you're worried and depressed. You wake in those cold dark hours just before dawn and all you can think of is how you wish you didn't have to face another day. Everything seems to be at its lowest ebb in these few hours, far more so than in the middle of the night. If dawn is just breaking the light is cold and grey – not ideal if you feel very down.

Unlike waking earlier on in the night it is really not worth making too many efforts to sleep again. Going through the hot drink, warm bath, relaxation routine now may make you fall into a very deep sleep indeed, which is fine as long as you don't have to get up an hour or so later.

So if you do wake any time after five o'clock lie quietly for a while. If you normally wake to the sound of an alarm, appreciate the quietness of waking naturally. As you lie in bed listen for noises and sounds of the world waking round you – birdsong, cars on the road – and remember that there are plenty of people who normally get up before dawn to work, and others, on night shift, who haven't yet gone to bed. So you are not alone.

Try to have positive thoughts about waking early. It gives you time to start your day at a slow pace. You can have a morning bath, a leisurely breakfast, time to yourself.

If you feel up to it throw on a T-shirt and track suit and take yourself off for an early morning jog or brisk walk round the block. On your way notice all the signs of a world in the midst of starting a new day. If you have always slept well till now, invariably leaping out of bed at the last moment, you may not even have been aware of such a world.

If you feel it's too early for breakfast make yourself a quick waking-up drink first – you can sit down to a proper meal later. Apart from the usual drinks of tea, coffee and orange juice you could try any of the following, which need extra preparation but make a change.

If you have a liquidiser or blender you can try varying the morning orange juice by mixing it with other ingredients. For instance, a glassful of orange, the juice of half a lemon and an egg white all whizzed up together make a very refreshing drink. Add the egg yolks as well as the white and whizz together to make a more nourishing version; for this, you'll probably need a little more lemon juice, some sugar to taste and a little water to dilute the thick mixture.

Also in a blender you can mix together half a pint of cold milk, one egg yolk and a couple of teaspoons of honey.

Make the most of the time you have to yourself before the day starts officially. Don't fall into the trap, unless you feel energetic, of doing chores around the home or catching up on work, unless you normally work really well first thing in the morning.

All the time bear in mind what night-time is supposed to achieve – rest for the body and mind. Although you have got up you still owe it to yourself to rest, to let yourself gently into this new day.

Of course you may still feel you can't face yet another day but each day is a growing process, and each night too. It's a growing towards acceptance of what is getting you down, and this is not something that can or even should be achieved quickly. If it is to be a lasting change, a change through which you will be able to develop and get to know yourself better, then it needs to be worked towards slowly and surely, using along the way all the various forms of comfort that you need.

Appendix – If You Need Help

Most of the suggestions contained in this book are easily put into practice. This is deliberate because when you are depressed you have very little mental or physical energy so for at least some of the time you need to be cushioned, helped along. The whole point about comfort is that it should be achieved with the minimum of effort.

But this section is designed to help if you simply have to act either to solve a specific problem or to put into practice an idea. If you were feeling fit and happy you would probably have both the energy and the enthusiasm to rush out and do your own research but the chances are that's the last thing you feel like doing at the moment. So, before your interest wanes or your problems get out of hand, here are some addresses, phone numbers and reading suggestions. Because facts and figures change so rapidly I have kept to well-known organisations rather than brand new ones, but established groups and societies are well equipped to deal with your queries and to refer you to more specialised groups if necessary. The most important point is that if you have the need or interest now, you should be able to pick up the telephone or write a letter to set things in motion.

If You Can't Cope

There are times when the way you feel or the problems that surround you suddenly get out of control and all the sensible reasoning in the world won't help. It is at that point that you will probably need to turn to experts for help, advice and support.

These days, there is a group for almost every problem you can think of, certainly far too many groups to list here. But those that are here can either help you themselves or put you in touch with the right sort of help.

The Samaritans. You will find the number of your local branch in the telephone directory, but if you haven't got a phone book to hand you can phone the well-known London number of 01-626 9000. People hesitate to contact them because they think they only deal with potential suicides. This is not the case. The Samaritans will listen to any problem, any time, day or night. They cannot provide instant solutions, and they are not there for that, but they can tell you where you can go for specific help, or can help you themselves just by listening as you sound off.

The Citizens Advice Bureau. If the crisis can wait until daytime, you should be able to find a branch near you, by looking in the phone book. The CAB can offer advice on all sorts of subjects – legal, emotional, financial, marital – and can also pass you on to specific groups for specialised help.

Alcoholics Anonymous can help heavy drinkers or potential alcoholics with counselling and group therapy. Head Office is at General Services Office, PO Box 1, Stonebow House, Stonebow, York YO1 2NP (0904 644026) but your local group will be in the phone book.

Al-Anon is part of the same group but is designed to help the families of alcoholics to understand the problem and cope with it. The headquarters can be found at 61 Great Dover Street, London SE1 4YF (01–403 0888).

Accept, at 200 Seagrave Road, London SW6 1RQ (01–381 3155), can refer you to therapists, detoxification centres, after-care help and so on. There are also leaflets and they can give you the address of a local counselling group.

Alcohol Concern, at 305 Grays Inn Road, London WC1X 8QF (01-833 3471), has centres offering advice all over the UK and provides a useful list of booklets and books on alcohol problems.

Gamblers Anonymous and **Gam-Anon** are both at 17–23 Blantyre Street, Cheyne Walk, London SW10 0DT (01–352 3060) and provide supportive help for gamblers and their families.

Compassionate Friends at 6 Denmark St, Bristol BS1 5QD (0272 292778), National Secretary: Jillian Tallon, can offer help and comfort to the bereaved – especially to parents who have lost children.

Turning Point at 9 Long Lane, London EC1 (01–606 3947), offers help to alcoholics and drug addicts. There are two centres in London but you can telephone them from outside their area and they will be able to put you in touch with a suitable group locally.

Release at 169 Commercial St, London E1 6BW (01–377 5905), can offer a great deal of help and support on the legal, social and medical problems of taking drugs. They can also take on psychological problems.

Mind, 22 Harley Street, London W1N 1AP (01–637 0741), is a national charity for mental and emotional problems, which can give advice or refer you to your nearest self-help group or clinic.

There are several organizations that can give advice about psychotherapy and offer sessions. You will have to pay but often the amount can be adjusted according to your means.

Institute of Psycho-Analysis, 63 New Cavendish Street, London W1 (01–580 4952).

London Centre for Psychotherapy, 19 Fitzjohns Avenue, Swiss Cottage, London NW3 5JY (01–435 0873).

The Winnicott Clinic of Psychotherapy, 12 The Crescent, London SW13 (01–878 4522).

If you feel that what might help is learning to relax there are a number of groups that can help either by attending a group or by using tapes.

Relaxation for Living, Amber Lloyd, Dunesk, 29 Burwood Park Road, Walton on Thames, Surrey KT12 5LH.

The Stress Syndrome Foundation, Cedar House, Yalding, Maidstone, Kent ME18 6JD (send s.a.e. for advice and information).

Lifeskills, 3 Brighton Road, Barnet, London N2 (01–346 9646). Self-help cassettes to help you control stress, tension and so on.

Society of Teachers of the Alexander Technique, 3 Albert Court, Kensington Gore, London SW7 (01–589 3834).

Finding a group

If you want to pin down a specific group without phoning them your local library should be able to help. An excellent book which lists a large number of self-help organisations is *The 'Someone to Talk to' Directory*, published by the Mental Health Foundation and distributed by Routledge and Kegan Paul. Your library should have a copy.

Getting Away From It All

Maybe you would like to take a break and leave your troubles behind you for a while. The right sort of holiday could do wonders for you, so here are some suggestions.

If money allows, a few days at a health farm is a real treat, and one which you deserve right now. From the moment you arrive you will be looked after, not just by having meals provided and beds made, but also by having your whole day organised and filled with steam baths, saunas, massages. Men as well as women benefit from this sort of treatment and you will come home not only feeling better but looking better too. (And of course it's a perfect way to tackle being overweight in surroundings free from the usual temptations.) There are plenty of health farms around, and some will allow you to come in for a full day's treatment if you live near enough and can't afford to stay overnight.

Here are three to be going on with

- **Champneys** of Tring, Hertfordshire.
- **Forest Mere Hydro**, Forest Mere, Liphook, Hampshire GU30 7JQ.
- **Shrubland Hall Health Clinic**, Coddenham, Ipswich, Suffolk IP6 9QH.

An activity holiday will stimulate you as well as giving you a rest. It is also, incidentally, a good way to meet people. You can go away for a week or longer or, if this is difficult to organise, you can take advantage of the dozens of weekend or mid-week courses available. You can study almost anything you care to think of – bridge, yoga, wildlife, potholing, ceramics, architecture. Your local library should have a list of courses in your area and your travel agent can give you a British Tourist Association leaflet with details of courses further afield. Or write to the **British Tourist Authority**, Queen's House, 64 St James's Street, London SW1A 1NF for a list of Holiday Courses. **The National Institute of Adult Education**, 19b Montfort Street, Leicester LE1 7GH, publishes an annual Calendar of Short Residential Courses which is very comprehensive.

If you are interested in the environment, you could go on one of the courses run by the **Field Studies Council**, Preston Montford, Montford Bridge, Shrewsbury SY4 1HW. The Council has nine centres all over the country and offers courses in subjects like plant identification, bird watching and archaeology.

Loughborough University runs a summer course each year which caters for every possible interest for both adults and children. It has a creche for under-fives if the only way you can get away is to take the children too. Write to Summer Programme, Centre for Extension Studies, Loughborough University, Leicestershire LE11 3TU for details.

Many centres cater for those interested in arts and crafts, and if most of your time is spent at a desk or doing brain work, it makes a soothing change to choose a holiday where you use your hands. **West Dean College**, near Chichester, West Sussex, offers a wide variety of courses in arts and crafts like jewellery-making, pottery and painting.

But if you don't want to do anything, or have anything done to you, a weekend or week in retreat may be the answer. You don't have to be religious to stay in a retreat, the cost is modest and few demands are made on you. Most of the time will be spent sleeping, praying, or talking quietly if you wish. In return you will get plain food in good quantities and comfortable if austere accommodation.

Some retreat houses are more organised than others but whatever the programme you will at least have a few days far away from everyday life – no newspapers, television or traffic.

There are three major co-ordinating bodies for retreats in Britain. When you write for information, do enclose a stamped addressed envelope.

- **The National Retreat Commission**, 7 Lance Lane, Liverpool 15, has information about the thirty or so Roman Catholic retreats.
- **The Association for Promoting Retreats**, Church House, Newton Road, London W2, has a similar list of Anglican retreat houses.
- **The Society of Friends**, Friends House, Euston Road, London NW1, has a list of Quaker retreats.

Most of the tour companies organise ordinary holidays where people alone are welcome, although, unless you are willing to share a room, you will usually have to pay a supplement for a single room. Your travel agent should be able to advise you on these holidays, as well as telling you about the special ones for singles.

Dateline International, 23 Abingdon Road, London W8 (01–938 1011) is not just a computer dating agency. It also produces a magazine *Select*, available at most newsagents, and organises holidays for singles. There are short-term holidays in this country and longer ones, over two weeks, abroad – and there is no age limit.

Saga, Senior Citizens Holidays Ltd, 119 Sandgate Road, Folkestone, Kent (0303 40000) has all sorts of holidays at home and abroad for the over-sixties.

Your Job and Career

Once you have made up your mind to change your job or your career or go back to studying and training, there should be no holding you back, provided you can get that basic start on information.

You may want to change direction but be unsure where to turn.

Some Jobcentres have an **Occupational Guidance Service** (your nearest centre will tell you where to go) which gives free advice.

If you don't mind paying for careers advice you can try any of the following.

- **Career Analysts**, Career House, 90 Gloucester Place, London W1H 4BL (01–935 5452).
- **The Independent Assessment and Research Centre**, 57 Marylebone High Street, London W1M 3AE (01–486 6106).
- **Vocational Guidance Centre**, 60 Fountain Street, Manchester M2 2FE (061–832 7671).

Unfortunately there is no central body to provide information on the hundreds of courses for GCE 'O' and 'A' levels and further education classes leading to certificates or degrees. Your best bet is to approach your nearest university, polytechnic, or further education institute for details.

Usually you will be able to choose to study full-time, part-time, or in the evenings but if none of these suits you can also take some courses by correspondence. Write to the **National Extension College**, Trumpington Street, Cambridge, for details.

If you are hovering on the edge of going back to work or college after years at home, look out for short courses designed to help you re-enter the world of work or study. They are usually called 'Fresh

Start' or 'New Horizons'. If your local Further Education College or Adult Education Centre doesn't offer such a course you may get one started if enough of you are willing to attend.

Most universities and polytechnics can waive normal entry requirements for mature students. Sometimes you may even be accepted for a degree course on interview alone, although you are more likely to be asked to produce an essay as well. Write to **UCCA (Universities Central Council on Admissions)**, PO Box 28, Cheltenham, Gloucestershire, for a booklet *How to Apply to University*. Have a look at the *Compendium of University Entrance Requirements* in your local library.

The Open University has no entry requirements at all. It operates more or less on a first come, first served basis. There is no time limit for completing a degree, you can even drop out for a year and come in again if necessary. Write for the free *Guide for Applicants to Open University*, the Open University, Walton Hall, Milton Keynes, MK7 6AA.

Financing your study may be a problem and the grants scene changes all the time. Best source of advice is the **National Union of Students**, or you can have a word with your local education authority.

Training for a new job or freshening up on an old skill is possible through the government **TOPS** scheme. There are over 600 courses to choose from and you are paid while you train. Ask at your local Jobcentre for details.

If you are approaching or are even past retirement age, this doesn't disqualify you from working or studying. There is no age limit on enrolling for an Open University course. There are also groups which specialise in careers and job advice for the older person.

Success After Sixty, 40–41 Old Bond Street, London W1, can give advice, mainly on office jobs.

Age Concern, Bernard Sunley House, 60 Pitcairn Road, Mitcham, Surrey CR4 3LL, can also advise and some of their branches run an employment service.

Useful Books

You will be able to choose books on specific career subjects in your library but there are some general books available that are worth looking at:

Equal Opportunities by Ruth Miller (Pengiun) is available at most libraries. It is an alphabetical guide to all sorts of careers, the training needed, prospects and pay.

A Compendium of Advanced Courses in Colleges of Further and Higher Education (Department of Education). Copies are available from your local careers office or education authority.

When You Are Left Alone

You could be alone for all sorts of reasons – widowhood, divorce, separation. In some cases it may be some time before the realisation hits you, and when it does you will want help of a practical kind at once, as well as all the comfort you can get.

Death is the last major social taboo. We prefer not to talk or think about it and when it happens to or affects those near us we can only accept a very limited amount of open grief.

This means that when death takes away someone close to you – a parent, a partner, or a child – you can feel even more bereft simply because those round you cannot comprehend your feelings and you may be afraid of embarrassing them by an overt show of pain.

Cruse is the National Organisation for the Widowed and their Children, Cruse House, 126 Sheen Road, Richmond, Surrey TW9 1UR (01–940 4818). It is an organisation for the widowed with over one hundred branches in Britain. They provide a counselling service, practical advice and social contact. Help is there at any stage and you can easily be put in touch with a local group.

There is also the **National Association of Widows**, 1st Floor, Neville House, 14 Waterloo Street, Birmingham B2 5TX (021–643 8348).

Two thousand babies a year die inexplicably in their cots – the **Foundation for the Study of Infant Deaths**, 15 Belgrave Square, London SW1X 8PS (01–235 1721), is there to help by talking and informing. The same applies to the **Stillbirth and Neonatal Deaths Association (SANDS)**, 28 Portland Place, London W1N 3DE (01–436 5881). Both can put you in touch with local people in a similar situation.

Outsiders often underestimate the trauma of a miscarriage – the fact that the emotional after-effects can last for months, even years. The **Miscarriage Association**, 18 Stoneybrook Close, West Bretton, Wakefield, West Yorkshire WF4 4TP, is a newish group that aims to set up a countrywide network of local groups and to give information and help.

When a marriage or relationship ends there are often more problems than the emotional ones, especially if children and a home are involved.

The **National Council for One Parent Families**, 255 Kentish Town Road, London NW5 2LX (01–267 1361) caters for all one-parent families. It can offer all sorts of practical advice and can put you in touch with a local group. There is also the **Scottish Council for Single Parents**, at 13 Gayfield Square, Edinburgh EH1 3NX (031–556 3899). **Singlehanded Limited**, Thorne House, Hankham Place, Stone Cross, Pevensey, East Sussex BN24 5ER (0323 767507), will endeavour to put one-parent families in touch with each other for mutual support and help. Membership £35.

Gingerbread, 35 Wellington Street, London WC2 7BN (01–240 0953) has more than 400 groups all over Britain. It can give advice over the phone, with leaflets or via local groups. It also runs a separate holiday section which offers really cheap holidays to single parents either at home or as far away as the States. Locally, the group will provide social activities and help with babysitting so that the single parent can get an occasional break.

Families Need Fathers, BM Families, London WC1 3XX (01–852 7123), is for fathers (and mothers) who are finding it hard to gain access to children after separation or divorce, and can give advice on custody problems.

The National Stepfamily Association, Ross Street Community Centre, Ross Street, Cambridge CB1 3BS (0223 215370) offers advice on all sorts of problems associated with stepparents and stepchildren.

Mothers Apart from their Children (MATCH), BM Problems, London WC1N 3XX, is a self-help group for mothers who have left not just their home but their children too.

Parents of Parents Eternal Triangle (POPETS), Mrs Shirley Hefferman, 15 Calder Close, Higher Compton, Plymouth PL3 6NT

(0752 777036), aims to help grandparents who have been denied access to their grandchildren following a separation or divorce.

If there has been cruelty to children, or if you suspect there has, the **National Society for the Prevention of Cruelty to Children (NSPCC)**, 67 Saffron Hill, London EC1N 8RS (01–242 1626) offers help and advice – anonymous if you prefer. **Childwatch**, 60 Beck Road, Everthorpe, Humberside, will give advice if you fear a child is being ill treated or abused.

Mothers of Abused Children, 25 Wampool Street, Silloth, Cumbria CA5 4AA (0965 31432) is a self-help group for mothers whose children have been the victims of incest.

Legal advice is often something a new single parent is most in need of. Many areas now have legal advice or neighbourhood law centres. For information about the nearest one to you contact **Legal Action Group**, 242 Pentonville Road, London N1 (01–833 3931).

If you miss an active social life but would feel more at ease with people with similar problems to your own, try the **National Council for the Divorced and Separated**, 13 High Street, Little Shelford, Cambridge CB2 5ES, or the **National Federation of Solo Clubs**, 7–8 Ruskin Chambers, 191 Corporation Street, Birmingham B4 6RP. Both have local groups offering social events such as dances and bingo. There is a membership fee and activities vary depending on the interests of local members. **National Federation of 18+ groups**, Nicholson House, Old Court Road, Newent, Gloucestershire (0531 821 210), organises social events for 18–30 years olds and has local groups. **Single And Loving It (SALI)**, Penny Moon, The Mint, Wallingford, Oxon (0491 33670), is a singles club with a difference – it is not designed for people to meet marriage partners. **NEXUS**, Nexus House, Blackstock Road, Finsbury Park, London N4 (01–359 7656/6703), specialises in introductions, meetings, group activities and has branches all over the country. Yearly membership fee is £61.20.

There is also a lonely-hearts tape service on 01–359 6321 – lonely people talk about themselves and would-be friends can get in touch. Tapes are changed once a week.

The Outsiders Club, Box 4ZB, London W1A 4ZB (01–499 0900) is especially for people who feel 'different' in some way – either because of disability or simply for emotional reasons. There are social events for members as well as a very helpful booklet on how to cope better.

Old Friends, 18a Highbury New Park, London N5 2DB (01–226 5432), is an agency catering specifically for the over-40s to find not just marriage partners but often friends of the same sex to go out with.

Many women these days find themselves looking after parents. Initially this may not affect their lives but as the parents become older and more demanding it may lead to giving up work and a gradual cut-off from everyday life. When the parent dies the isolation is complete. The **National Council for Carers and their Elderly Dependants**, 29 Chilworth Mews, London W2 3RG (01–724 7776), exists to fight for the rights of these single women and can also offer a tremendous amount of advice and support if needed.

Getting Fit, Looking Good

You are probably quite capable of getting out and starting a sport on your own, but it may help to have some extra information so that you can contact a local group of like-minded people who can help to spur you on.

Simple exercises can of course be done at home, alone, but if this doesn't appeal contact the **Keep Fit Association**, 16 Upper Woburn Place, London WC1 (01–387 4349). They will be able to tell you what classes are available in your area or give you names of local teachers. If you live in a remote area they can also provide you with good leaflets.

Should you prefer not to walk alone, **The Ramblers' Association**, 1–5 Wandsworth Road, London SW8 (01–582 6826), not only campaigns for footpath rights but also has many local groups which meet for organised rambles at weekends and holidays.

A little more energetic is fell walking. Details from the **British Mountaineering Council**, Crawford House, Precinct Centre, Booth Street East, Manchester M13 9RZ (061–273 5835).

Orienteering is a sort of adult paperchase. You need to build up stamina to run the course and you also need to learn to map read, but you can acquire both these skills in time and it is challenging and fun. More information from the **British Orienteering Federation**,

Riversdale, Dale Road North, Darley Dale, Matlock, Derbyshire DE4 2JB (0629 734042).

The Sports Council, 16 Upper Woburn Place, London WC1 (01–388 1277), offers all kinds of courses in mountain climbing, canoeing and so on, for absolute beginners as well as the more experienced.

The Cyclists Touring Club, Cotterell House, 69 Meadrow, Godalming, Surrey GU7 3HS (048–68 7217), can advise you on the type of bike you need. It can also put you in touch with a local group if you want company on your bike rides.

For swimming information contact the **Amateur Swimming Association**, Harold Fern House, Derby Square, Loughborough, Leicestershire LE11 OAL (0509 230431). It runs a scheme to encourage adults to swim and has a series of awards to keep your enthusiasm going. Your local swimming pool will also have details.

Yoga is so popular that you should have little difficulty in finding a local group, and your reference library will have a list of local societies. If you cannot find any classes, there are several books on the subject, try *Yoga* by James Hewitt in the Teach Yourself series, *Wake Up To Yoga* by Lynn Marshall, published by Ward Lock, or *Yoga Self-Taught* by André van Lysbeth, published by Unwin Paperbacks.

When it comes to pampering your body you may be lucky enough to have a good health shop close by where you can buy oils and herbs. If not, there are several mail order firms that offer a very wide selection.

The Body Shop, PO Box 24, Rustington, West Sussex BN16 3AT (0903 776151).

Aromatic Oil Co., 12 Littlegate Street, Oxford. You are welcome to call in as well as order by post.

John Bell & Croyden, 54 Wigmore Street, London W1H 0AU (01–935 5555), have a vast selection of oils and herbs as well as creams and ingredients for making your own cosmetics.

Culpeper Ltd., Hadstock Road, Linton, Cambridge (0223 891196), has branches in London, Brighton and Norwich. Enclose an s.a.e. when writing for a catalogue.

The best way to track down your nearest supplier for fresh herbs is to write, with an s.a.e., to **The Herb Society**, 77 Great Peter St, London SW1, or phone (01–222 3643).

If your weight is a problem and you've tried alone and failed, you might be more successful on a **Weight-watchers** therapy course. Find out about a local class from their head office at 635 Ajax Avenue, Slough (0753 70711). Maybe having to pay to lose weight will inspire you. There is also a self-help group, **Slimmers Anonymous**, The Manor House, Gravesend, Kent (047–482 (Shorne) 2853) where you can be put in touch with a local helper.

Help With Money

If you don't know very much about money or a crisis hits you, or you just want to make a better impression on your bank manager when you see him by seeming to have a grasp of the basics, you can go elsewhere for information before approaching the bank. You will obviously need to look elsewhere if you haven't got a bank account, too.

The Citizens Advice Bureau (number in the phone book) can help with financial advice, especially on what to do if a loan has been called in or your building society is threatening to foreclose on your mortgage.

The Department of Health and Social Security (see local phone book) can also help if you have problems over a low income and debts. Many people qualify for extra benefits and don't claim them because they don't realise their rights. It never does any harm to ask and even if you don't come away with cash you may find you qualify for other kinds of help.

Your local **tax office** is not necessarily a place to avoid. Again, many people pay too much tax simply because they don't fill out their tax returns properly (equally, others pay too little but we keep quiet about them!). Your tax office can help you fill out forms and make sure you don't pay too much – you may even get a rebate.

If you are self-employed and have never had an accountant it may make sense to have one. He could save you at least double his charges. Find a local qualified person by getting a list from the **Institute of Chartered Accountants**, Moorgate Place, London EC2, for England and Wales, and 24 Holborn, London EC1, for Scotland.

Books on money overflow from the shelves of every library and bookshop – how to save it, how to spend it, how to make it. Two that are crammed with advice and basic information are the *Save and Prosper Book of Money*, published by Collins, and *The Which? Book of Money* – this is available from the Consumers' Association Subscription Department, Caxton Hill, Hertford SG13 7LZ. A subscription to *Which?* magazine entitles you to take out a further subscription for the quarterly supplement *Money Which?*, which has an annual Tax Saving Guide and gives plenty of general information about all aspects of family finance.

Index